THE NEW THINKER'S LIBRARY

General Editor: RAYMOND WILLIAMS

LOVE

LOVE

BY

ROSEMARY HAUGHTON

LONDON
C. A. WATTS & CO. LTD.
1970

First published 1970

©

Rosemary Haughton

SBN: 296 34712 4

Printed in Great Britain by
Alden & Mowbray Ltd
at the Alden Press, Oxford
36/633

PREFACE

IT would not be difficult to fill a medium-sized library with books about love. There are books attempting to define it, and books telling us how to do it, whether in the nursery, in church or in bed. Of all important human words it has been used, and abused, in more varied senses than any other. It can describe a range of behaviour from sanctity to Sade and also what I feel about strawberries and cream. This short book is neither a dictionary of love, an atlas, nor a recipe book. Within its restricted scope it simply tries to give some impression of the vast range of human behaviour which can be related to the concept of love. Without taking any fixed notion of love as a starting point, a real definition (it can never be an exact one) is allowed to emerge, through the evidence of writers and of ordinary people as they work out ways of living together. There can be no last word on such a subject, but only a lifelong deepening of experience and understanding of love, or else a gradual loss of sensitivity to what it stands for. But I hope that by the time the reader gets to the end of the book he or she will find it considerably more difficult to use the word 'love' without meaning anything much at all.

R.H.

July, 1969

v

CONTENTS

THE author and publishers are grateful to the following who have kindly granted permission to use copyright material:

Messrs Valentine, Mitchell & Co. (*Diary of Ann Frank*); the author and Macmillan & Co. Ltd (Ann Cornelisen, *Torregreca*); the authors and Sheed & Ward Ltd (Terence Eagleton, *The New Left Church* and Herbert McCabe, *Law, Love and Language*); the author and Penguin Books Ltd (Leila Berg, *Risinghill: Death of a Comprehensive School*).

I

ATTITUDES TO LOVE IN
CHILD-REARING

But what if man had eyes to see the true beauty – the divine beauty,
I mean, pure and clear and unalloyed, not clogged with the pollu-
tions of mortality and all the colours and vanities of human life –
thither looking and holding converse with the true beauty human
and divine? Remember how in that communion only, beholding
beauty with the eye of the mind, he will be enabled to bring forth,
not images of beauty, but realities (for he has hold not of an image
but of a reality) and bringing forth and nourishing true virtue to
become the friend of God and be immortal, if mortal man may.
Would that be an ignoble life?

THUS Socrates described man's highest desire, or at least this
is how Plato describes him describing it, in what is possibly the
most famous of his Dialogues. The *Symposium* has acquired an
unexpected fame recently, by edging its way into the market
for pseudo-pornographic paperbacks, suggestively accompany-
ing the *Kama Sutra*. I doubt if Plato would have been pleased,
but it is a fitting punishment, for the high-flown, portentous
silliness of much of the *Symposium* is well matched by the
hilariously serious silliness of the *Kama Sutra*, product of a
culture which, on this evidence, must have been intensely and
self-engrossedly dying of boredom. Both compositions,
however, claim to be concerned with love.

Possibly, the authors of both had their tongues in their
cheeks. But if Plato hadn't, and was reporting a real conversation, then certainly his Aristophanes had, in his space-fiction
account of the origins of sexuality in the division, by jealous
gods, of the hitherto spherical human beings into two halves,

I

which ever since strive to come together again. Meanwhile the gods had mercifully allowed the genital organs and faces to switch round to the flat side of the creatures, thus facilitating their attempts at temporary re-unification. Hence sex, with all its miseries and frustrations.

Aristophanes presumably wasn't being serious, and Socrates tried to restore some sense to a singularly foolish discussion by first debunking some exalté and unrealistic notions about love, and then trying to explain what love is *really* for. Beauty is what men chiefly desire, and in the passage quoted he describes the highest kind of beauty, the ultimate felicity, therefore, that man can desire. These words he gives as a quotation from his teacher Diotima, but, he adds, 'I am persuaded of their truth.' And at this point he shows the real place of love in human life. 'And being persuaded of them, I try to persuade others, that in the attainment of this end human nature will not easily find a better helper than love. And therefore, also, I say that every man ought to honour him as I myself honour him and walk in his ways, and exhort others to do the same, and praise the power and spirit of love according to the measure of my ability now and ever.'

This task that Socrates set himself has been undertaken by very many since then, and this book is written for the same purpose. Socrates refused to accept definitions of love, but preferred to point out its usefulness. I shall not begin with a definition, but rather accept the loose popular use of the word, which is ill-defined in general but used in particular instances with a perfectly clear meaning, though the meaning may vary. And I hope that by examining the way in which love happens, or is prevented, and the way in which people react to it when it does occur, a closer understanding of its nature may emerge and some notion of why this thing that men profess to value is, in practice, so carefully suppressed, evaded or distorted.

The obvious place to start is at the beginning of human life, when the child is being moulded to fit his particular society. It is during the early years, even the early months, that the patterns of emotional development are laid down, though we shall see that human beings do not always conform to the desired forms and that this fact is one of the most significant in any investigation into the nature of love.

It is a cliché of modern psychology that most adult delinquency and social maladjustment derives from some degree of inability to form true relationships. People who cannot love are warped human beings, according to this doctrine, and this inability is usually directly traceable to the kind of experience undergone by the child, sometimes so early in life that all trace of it has disappeared from memory. There is some evidence that experiences at, or shortly after, birth, can so inhibit a child emotionally that he becomes autistic, that is, unable to form any relationship whatever with another human being, remaining wholly self-absorbed unless patient and knowledgeable care is lavished on him, often for years, in order to create the fragile channels of human communications that were so tragically cut off. This extreme of the inability to love is so odd as to be frightening and repellent to ordinary people. It seems possible, indeed, that autism is responsible for the old stories of changelings, children who appeared human but were really fairies, having no human feelings and probably evil in their intentions. The fact that this extreme case is so upsetting to ordinary people is interesting, for this reaction does not necessarily follow from any *conscious* notion that the ability to love is necessary for human beings. Since this inability to form relationships – which is what we normally mean by loving – is so repellent when encountered, it might be thought that the opposite, a capacity to form many and close relationships, in fact to love fully and easily, would be desired and admired. In theory, in certain cultures, this has been and is so. But not only does the actual practice contradict the modern theory that the ability to love is an unqualified good, but many cultures reject the notion, in theory and practice, even as an ideal. Even when love is regarded as desirable it is severely restricted, either in the people whom it is proper to love, or in the degree to which they may be loved, or in the ways in which love may be shown. In fact the study of child care, both in the past and present, is largely a study of the restriction or suppression of love. To love too much or too exclusively, or the wrong person, is often a worse offence than to fail in love towards those whom it is proper to love. Juliet, for instance, was much to blame for loving the wrong person. If she had shown but little affection for her parents they might have been disappointed, but would not have regarded her failure as a grave offence.

The Manus men of New Guinea would not dream of loving their wives. Love, or rather a kind of easy-going loyalty, is restricted to the brother and sister relationship, but lack of intensity even here is usual. Love, in fact, is normally regarded as dangerous, and if not wholly outlawed it must be strictly controlled. This is apparent even at the infant stage, and the patterns of child care are in many cases self-perpetuating. The grown-up child treats his or her own children in the same way as he or she was once treated, not only because that is the custom, but because the type of treatment produces psychological reactions that dictate that kind of behaviour to the children.

The one really constant element in the endless variety of methods of suppressing or restricting love in children is that these methods are not wholly successful. Yet this lack of success in some cases is *approved*. It can happen that in the same cultures whose customs seem to be aimed at suppression of love, the outbreak and triumph of love may be celebrated in poetry or story. Two very different types of culture can be used to show this.[1]

The medieval cult of chivalry demanded that a boy of noble birth be removed from his parents' home at the age of seven, and reared in an honourable but arduous servitude in the household of some other nobleman. Even before this, he was constantly drilled in the arts of war, in endurance and in forms of courtesy. His demeanour towards his parents was expected to be one of total submission and elaborate reverence and this attitude was further reinforced in the household that took over his education. The goal of all this was knighthood, in which the human attachments so carefully suppressed were to be directed to God, the King, and the Lady, whoever she might be. Although this last was a real woman, the Lady of the young knight's devotion occupied the position of goddess, and devotion to her therefore did not conflict with the demands of feudal loyalties. This arrangement could be expected to disinfect marriage and family life of any embarrassingly strong affection which might interfere with the knight's usefulness to his overlord, or prevent the smooth production of further little knights, equally detached from the ties of earthly and earthy affection. In this case the contemporary stories on the whole reflect the accepted patterns of behaviour, yet the notion that it is possibly risky to ritualize love to this extent can be detected in such tales as that of Lancelot and Guinevere, where devotion to the Lady gets out of hand and definitely does interfere with knightly allegiance. The moral verdict is decidedly ambiguous, but popular feeling has always tended to take the lovers' part. In a different vein,

[1] For many examples used in this chapter I have drawn heavily on the work of Margaret Mead, especially in *Male and Female*, and also a collection edited by her, by various psychologists and anthropologists under the title *Childhood in Contemporary Cultures* (University of Chicago Press, 1955).

there is *Sir Orfeo*, a curious composition set in England but probably derived from a Breton version, which shows a passionate devotion between husband and wife. Real life has also preserved stories of the heroic love of married people, such as the story, beloved of English nurseries, of the devotion of his queen to Richard Lionheart. Love has a way of breaking through the constraints set upon it by early training, and over and over again popular tales celebrate this fact. These were the stories and songs that children, reared in the tradition of chivalry, heard told and sung from their earliest years. This is one of these curious contradictions in human behaviour about love that will become increasingly obvious. Love is feared and prized, restricted and celebrated. It is dangerous and yet essential.

The children of Bali are systematically discouraged from allowing the full development of emotion in ordinary life. Their feelings are provoked by grown-ups, who encourage them to join in games, then leave them flat before the high point of the game is reached. Children are constantly stimulated by patting and caresses, then left to make the best of their unsatisfied and chaotic feelings. Mothers borrow a baby from another family in order to provoke a child's jealousy, and when he is roused to rage and misery, laugh at him. Margaret Mead notes, 'Little children are not permitted to quarrel, they are not allowed to struggle over toys, or pull or claw at each other, there are always the elders there to separate them, gently, impersonally and inexorably and so completely that over two years of living in a Balinese village I never saw two children or adolescents fight. The emotion, as before, is not worked out but simply halted.' The children soon learn not to respond to such stimuli; they become withdrawn and emotionally unresponsive, acquiring that air of dispassionate wisdom that is so much admired by westerners. This suppression of emotional response is so profound that children will sink into a trance-like sleep when situations of danger or uncertainty occur. Margaret Mead writes: 'During child-birth in a tiny one-room home, or after an accident for which one may be blamed, children and older people also fall into a deep sleep from which it is difficult to rouse them.'

But the need to reach out into the strange regions of beauty and love can seldom be entirely denied, and here again the culture itself makes provision for this, through ritual plays and dances and the making of music. Colin McPhee, in the book referred to, gives an account of the formation of a traditional Balinese orchestra by a group of boys, some as young as seven. The concentration, the passionate intensity of these children as they learn to play complicated music is something that would only be paralleled among European children in the case of a few gifted individuals, yet these were a chance group of ordinary village boys. The need to break free of the limits of normal experience finds an outlet here, and is all the stronger because of its suppression in the area of human relationships.

The compensatory character of art for the Balinese is even more clearly shown in their ritual drama. Margaret Mead emphasizes the extraordinary continuity between everyday life and the dance and drama which are so important to these people. Everyone takes part at certain stages of life, and little girls of three can be seen practising the elaborate hand gestures of the traditional story-dances. All the emotions that the child is forbidden to display or ever feel in everyday life are transposed into the parallel life of ritual drama, and worked out there with explicitness and power, but always within the safe limits of the traditional forms. This 'disinfecting' of normal emotion will be found to be a recurrent theme in the story of the attempts to deal with the power of love.

It is noticeable that the stories enacted in Balinese plays are mostly concerned with themes of anger and revenge. There are many battles, and the chief characters are a dragon and a witch, the latter an exaggeratedly female figure who represents all the malevolence of the feminine as it appears in myths the world over. There is little room for what we might regard as manifestations of love, such as devotion to the beloved, or gentleness or self-sacrifice. It seems at first sight that these ritual outlets have nothing to do with love, or its suppression, since it is ignored. But in fact this absence of anything that characterizes what we call love is important, because it shows something that will become increasingly apparent, that love is not a separate form of human emotion or reaction, on a par with anger, fear, desire, ambition, and so on. It can more nearly be described, even at this stage, as a drive towards an experience of life that transcends what is normally available, as Socrates' words indicated. But Socrates' presentation of it is serene and this serenity is taken for granted because it is assumed in this context that the pursuit of this high goal will be undertaken by civilized people, with well-organized lives, and that they will be encouraged, or at least not hindered. But it is already clear that this 'drive' is more often regarded with fear and suspicion, or sometimes with a religious awe. But if the resulting suppression of this drive is extreme the outlets that are found do not allow it to take a form we would call love, because there is no scope for this expression of it. In that case it seems to take aggressive and vengeful forms, as if to break through by violence. This transformation of love into anger and destructiveness is a common theme of fairy tales, where a lover scorned by a heartless lady and finally winning her, despises her and punishes her for refusing him. Love, as Socrates points out, is not an end, or a clear-cut emotion, but rather an activity directed towards an end, and the nature of the activity can be distorted out of all recognition. But the concept 'love' is important, because it signifies the nature of the activity which is capable of reaching the goal.

When it is distorted it is still intensely powerful but it does *not* reach the goal. So, in the Balinese culture, music and ritual drama provide an outlet for suppressed emotion, but none of it leads to further personal development. All it does is to work out harmlessly the radical frustration of all emotion in young children and adults. The training in chivalry, while it restricted love between parents and children and between man and wife, did at least propose as an ideal the love of a woman, even though it was a conventional and canalized love. Also the stories and songs provided an acceptable fantasy world which was concerned with love, and did direct emotion towards that 'region' where love seemed to lead the heroic lovers of legend.

An example from nearer home may help to show how the frustration of love can be organized throughout a whole culture, and lead not only to the virtual outlawing of love in the Socratic sense but to a widespread restriction of the meaning of the word itself, in line with this frustration.

The book already quoted contains a study of French child-care patterns. (In this case it is possible for many people to verify the observations of these trained researchers from their own more casual experience.) It should be noticed that this essay concerns French customs and patterns of some ten years ago. The style of life in France is already drastically changing and this is interesting, because it shows how difficult it is totally to suppress the fundamental drive which we call love.

An essay by Martha Wolfenstein gives a minute description of the behaviour of French children in a Paris park. The children come with their mother, or some other guardian, and they are expected to stay with this family group. A small child will often spend his time playing in the sand by the bench where his mother or grandmother sits, and contact with children of other families is discouraged, though not normally forbidden.

Toys too, are very much family property, and will be re-
claimed at once if 'borrowed'. Likewise, the toys of another
family will be promptly returned, with apologies – to the
parent, not to the child, for the toy is regarded as the adult's
property. There is constant discouragement of physical
effort or of any degree of loud talk or laughter. Children are
exhorted to be gentle, to 'stop now', to 'leave him alone', and
there is great emphasis on keeping clean. Children are also
expected to sit still for long periods. The ideal child seems to
be one who is obedient, almost silent, uninterested in other
children, and whose play is almost entirely with his hands.
Children learn to be active in talk – though quietly – rather
than in movement, and arguments are pursued almost for
their own sake, without reaching, or wanting to reach, any
conclusion.

Play, in fact, is regarded as a trivial occupation, to be
restricted so that it does not inconvenience adults. And this
practical contempt for children as people, whose foolish needs
have to be tolerated but kept within strict bounds, is shown
even more strongly in the affectionate contempt that French
parents show for their children's strong feelings. Miss Wolfenstein describes a scene where a boy of about six was spanked
by his mother. She then returned to her husband and baby,
ignoring the little boy's angry and mortified sobs. He walked
about for a while, miserable and tense, and attracted the
attention of several adults, but his own mother scarcely
glanced at him and was smiling contentedly. Finally, as
children will after a row, the boy came back to her, longing
to be reconciled, and clung to her, burying his head in her lap.
She embraced him kindly, but laughed in an amused way and
joked about him to another woman. It was clear that the
boy's feelings did not seem to her at all important. This
incident is paralleled by others showing the same tolerant
indifference to children's feelings. Children are not really

people, they are only preparing to be people, and meanwhile they must be trained not to interfere with the concerns of the real (grown-up) world.

Other studies show the same attitude in relation to school work. Children are expected to work long hours at boring work, because this is necessary to prepare them for a financially successful future. Lessons must be *sérieux* and their tedium, and their power to exhaust the child, are virtually the required proof that what goes on at school really is *sérieux*. Progressive schools and teaching methods have made little headway in France, at least until recently, because methods of teaching that the children enjoy are equated by the parents with play, and play is *pas sérieux*.

French parents are not given to showing appreciation of their children's existence, any more than of their achievements, which are smilingly dismissed as unimportant. The usual line is one of complaint at the amount of anxiety, work, and expense the child causes his parents. A child's business is not to enjoy life, and nobody expects to enjoy him. His whole task is to prepare arduously for grown-up life by working hard at school, and to be as little trouble as possible. He must be clean, quiet, polite and generally unobtrusive, and in the interests of this he must learn to tolerate a great deal of boredom. In an extremely illuminating definition, Miss Wolfenstein sums up the French ideal of being *bien élevé*: 'To be well brought up – *bien élevé* – means to be able to be bored in the family circle without protesting overtly.'

But where is all this boredom leading? Older French adolescents do not have the reputation of being repressed – in fact their sexual conduct is, and is expected to be, fairly easy-going. French adults demand, as of right, a great deal of pleasure both in food and sex, and it is considered perfectly normal for a respectable married man to have a mistress as well, because unless his wife is unusually gifted sexually he might run short of sexual pleasure, which is a deprivation no one could seriously expect him to tolerate. His wife, on the other hand, is expected to cook very well indeed, and will normally spend on food a proportion of the family income that English or American housewives would consider fantastic.

The restricted and emotionally discounted child is in fact being tacitly informed that if he works hard enough and submits thoroughly to adults, now, he will acquire the kind of job and status which will make it possible for him to enjoy adult pleasures as much as he likes. This is the aim, and it is pursued with all possible *sérieux*.

Here is another type of the displacement of love. This time the drive towards transcendent experience is not discharged in the form of ritualized anger and revenge, but in the form of the pursuit – and achievement – of pleasure. In neither case are personal relationships the 'locus' of the experience, except incidentally. The pleasure is a personal and private one, and this is to be expected as the result of an early training that tends to isolate the child, not allowing him to relate in any deep or satisfying way to the adults who control his destiny. The only form of child love that seems to be allowed is that between children of the same family, or occasionally between children of different families who themselves are friendly. This devotion can become very strong, but it is fated to give way to the pleasure-ideal of adult life, for such childhood and adolescent devotions are treated with the same tolerant amusement as children's rages or loves. They are not *sérieux* and have no place in 'real' life which is devoted to pleasure, and to money as the means to it. There is a kind of fatalism in the French adolescent's attitude to his love affairs which is absent in English and American 'teenagers, who hope – however unrealistically – that falling in love will lead to marriage – if not this time then next. To the French 'teenager, marriage is in a different category. It is *sérieux*.

But, as in the case of the ballads and tales of the Middle Ages, the artistic comment on the social situation reveals more than the conscious assumptions of the people concerned. Films about children uncover both an understanding of the real depth of childish emotion, and an implacable cynicism about the place of such feelings in human life. This cynicism in its turn justifies the kind of child-care that makes it inevitable. The best French films have a well deserved reputation for psychological sensitivity and a remorseless realism about human emotions. What is considered to be 'real' in any culture is a good indication of the categories of feeling that are excluded, taboo – that is 'unreal'. The French form of child-training excludes childish passion as *pas sérieux*, but French films show these passions are extremely powerful, yet inevitably useless and merely miserable, thus justifying, in a devious way, their 'taboo' character in ordinary life. In the book mentioned, French films about children are contrasted with Italian, English and American ones in which, though in varying ways, the emotions and desires of children are shown to lead to some real catharsis. There may be tragedy, but there is meaning and purpose in the child's devotion. *Whistle down the Wind* is about a child's mistaken devotion, but the devotion is real and tragic and alters the course of events. *The Fallen Idol* shows a boy whose devotion nearly leads his hero to trial for a murder he did not commit, but in the end all is well. The boy's feelings matter, they are effective.

The moral of the French film is different. In an episode of *The Seven Deadly Sins* a girl of thirteen works up a fantasy in which she thinks she is pregnant by an artist staying in the hotel her mother keeps because she sat in a chair which was still warm with his body. This pathetic bid for adult possession of the mysteries of sex is gradually uncovered by her mother's questions. The man is present, and both laugh at her and assure her she is not pregnant, leaving her mortified and bereft of her dream. But the mother uses this encounter as a spring board to an affair of her own with the artist, and incidentally she tells him of her own adolescent dream of a great love. But this is a casual affair for both, for the intensity of a child's feelings are not for them.

Another film, *The Male Brute*, shows a little boy's passionate devotion to his mother who is a prostitute. He is desperately jealous of one of her lovers, and she cannot take him seriously, though she is fond of him. The film acknowledges explicitly the heroic single-mindedness and tragic depth of a child's love, but it leads nowhere. It has no future – sad, but that's how things are. 'Realism', here, means the assumption that love like this is inevitably futile. In *The Red Balloon* the child's world is beautiful and complete, but utterly divorced from the 'real' world. The ending shows the boy lifted up into the sky by hundreds of coloured balloons, symbolizing very clearly the 'unreal', 'out of this world' nature of childish ideas and feelings.

So although the artistic comment on the social situation reveals the existence of true love it only reinforces the practical conclusions that are evident in the methods of bringing up children. All this emotion is useless, we will settle for pleasure, of which sexual pleasure is the most obvious kind, and concentrate on that.

In the pursuit of this extremely logical course, the word love itself has been adapted in meaning in order to assist the process. *L'amour* is even more specifically sexual in reference than 'love' has become in the Anglo-Saxon cultures, and refers almost exclusively to the exchange of sexual pleasure. The adult French are not romantic, and the French enthusiasm for *l'amour* in this restricted sense has helped to restrict the meaning of the word in other European cultures also. In England especially it has become fashionable to admire the 'realism' of the French in this matter.

This deference of English intellectuals to the French notion of 'realism' is an interesting indication of the kind of shift in social patterns in England which has been going on since the war. The 'romantic' tradition became weaker. The futility of deep feeling was accepted, and the pursuit of pleasure was seen as reasonable in a basically hopeless and ridiculous situation. This is already changing and French influence is now almost nil, but while it lasted it was almost unquestioned.

This tendency in English literature naturally raises questions about the type of child-care inflicted on these writers. If my thesis is useful at all, there should be some correlation between the two. There is not sufficient research material available yet for a clear verdict, but two facts are interesting. One is that this 'realism' of a pseudo-French type (with a characteristically English cosiness added to it, rather incongruously) emanates almost exclusively from 'intellectuals' whose background is middle class. The newer writers, with a different background, are free to take a different view of life. The middle-class way of life is much more sharply differentiated from that of the working classes in England than in France, where children of all kinds normally go to the same schools and, unless they are very poor or very rich, at least aim at the same standards of being *bien-élevé*. In England the new 'realism' did not spread to people of working-class origin to any great extent. (Books about working-class life seem mostly to be written by, and for, middle-class people, possibly 'new' ones.) The older, more romantic tradition about love-relations subsists in working-class communities, though laced with a bracing dose of commonsense about sex, and a 'realism' of a more homely and brutal kind. Courtships are still often 'steady' and are intended to lead to marriage, though there is probably a lot more experiment first. Still, the experiments are regarded as a preliminary to a love-match, not to the abandonment of love. This is not the ethos that produces the world of, for instance, Simon Raven.

The other fact, paralleling the class separation in England and the allied cultural differences, is that child-care has also been radically different in different classes. This is much less so now, but before and during the war (when most of the present generation of writers were babies) the working classes still went in for hit or miss, rough but basically affectionate type of child-care. Children might be spanked or even leathered, and babies given chocolate, crisps, tea and ice cream, to quiet them, but they stood a good chance of being loved, and babies in particular got a lot of cuddling, were nursed and admired by all the women of the family, and probably by the neighbours as well. Fathers and brothers also could play with the baby without embarrassment though older boys might resent being asked to 'mind' him. They were picked up when they cried (if only because in a cramped home the noise is intolerable), dandled, spoiled and given 'comforters'.

Middle-class babies, on the other hand, almost all suffered to some degree from the influence of Doctor Truby King, whose teaching on child-care has caused more suffering to both mothers and children than many a monster of sadism. His baneful influence on middle-class nurseries is only rivalled by that of the evangelical doctrine of infant depravity, which caused one devoted Victorian mother to whip her four months old baby 'until I could not whip him any more' in an attempt to subdue his rebellious spirit. Although Doctor King did not advise beating, he considered that infants must be made to conform to the norms of adult society in the matter of meal-times, hours of sleep and bowel functioning. Therefore the good mother should never feed her baby until the appointed time, however much he cried. After the first weeks he must not be fed at night, either, though it was permitted to change his nappies and attend to other 'real needs'. Here 'real' is, as usual, used to denote socially permissible feelings. A baby's soiled nappy indicated a 'real' need since faeces are socially unacceptable. His cries for signs of love were to be ignored – these were not 'real' needs. Since the display of such violent emotional hunger is not permissible for adults it must be taboo even in babies – that is, it must not exist, it is 'not real'. The baby was also to be given only the amount of food that was 'good for him', and no more. He was to be 'held out' on his pot before and after every feed, however much he protested.

So a whole generation of mothers tried to shut their ears to the sounds of babies crying. A generation of well-to-do infants sobbed themselves into a sleep of exhaustion after hours of fear and loneliness and despair, for the feelings of babies are as strong as those of grown-ups, and much more frightening because babies lack the means for understanding or control. Many of these babies were consistently undernourished, and cried from hunger – which was regarded as another form of baby 'naughtiness'. When the wretched infant was finally picked up and fed (if he wasn't too exhausted to feed properly at all) his comfortable sleepiness afterwards was interrupted by his being dumped inexorably on a cold pot. (This was done from birth!)

It would be very odd if this kind of treatment left no mark on the children. If a child's earliest experiences in relation to his mother are of loneliness, hunger, discomfort and frustration, this makes a close and comfortable relationship difficult. Besides, the insistence on discipline – especially in toilet training – and routine, and a god-like detachment on the mother's part in order to enforce (calmly and without anger) the routine and the discipline, meant that the barrier between mother and child did not easily become less as time went on. The children's books of this period, notably those by Arthur Ransome and his many plagiarists, show middle-class children who regard their parents as kind and just but essentially irrelevant to the real concerns of childhood. For the purposes of the story they are usually abroad, ill, dead, or thought to be dead. The need to have a consciously pleasant and respected notion of parents is thus conveniently reconciled with the unconscious desire for revenge. This is a far cry from the close, tempestuous, erratic, often resentful, but deeply emotional ties between working-class children and their parents. There are emotional malformations here, too, but not of the same kind.

When such early training was followed by boarding school at seven or eight, it is not really strange if the result is a genera- tion of emotionally inhibited people, distrustful of a love too often denied, and profoundly cynical about any motives but those leading to immediate personal satisfaction. It is possible, too, that the note of fantasy and adventure in the English attitude to casual sex, as distinct from the French attitude to pleasure which is essentially *sérieux* however bizarre in its manifestations, is due to the fact that English schooling, even the strictest, has suffered much less from the moral value placed on boredom. The English schools syllabus has left room for fantasy in the form of literature lessons, essays, and also the encouragement of free play in spare time, with opportunities for endless 'pretend' games, whose subjects were often drawn from history or story – the *Jungle Books*, *Treasure Island*, and many beloved 'cowboy' stories.

It would be a mistake to draw conclusions too confidently from such comparisons. Little systematic work has been done in this field, yet the comparisons I have made are suggestive, especially when put side by side with other well-documented examples of the correlation between child care patterns and the emotional development of adults.

An extreme example, for instance, of a restrictive and hostile pattern of child care roughly similar to that which Doctor Truby King preached with such disastrous success is to be found in a tribe observed by Margaret Mead, and reported in her book *Male and Female*. In this tribe sexual relations between husband and wife occur as the climax of a fight involving real antagonism, and are brief and brutal. The attitudes of parents to their children are similarly hostile. The baby's desire for the breast is regarded as an attack, and he is fed grudgingly, without cuddling or any more physical contact than is strictly necessary, and given only as much food as will serve to satisfy the worst of his hunger. He is left to cry for some time and is never fed until he is very hungry. When he is a little older, feeding becomes even more of a fight, and the child is pushed away roughly as soon as he has taken what his mother feels should be sufficient. The adults of the tribe are notably aggressive in their attitudes to the opposite sex, and also to other tribes. There is a close 'club' relationship, however, between members of the same sex, and the men, especially, enjoy life and laugh a great deal. (The English sense of humour is perhaps less a uniquely Anglo-Saxon phenomenon than we had imagined.) They are also courageous and resourceful, qualities which English middle-class culture esteems highly under the heading of 'qualities of leadership'. This is the ethos that made the British Empire, as it made the Roman one. The Spartans, using a similar technique of child-care, overdid the physical hardening bit and produced a class of immensely courageous nit-wits, which eventually defeated the object of the exercise.

There is one interesting difference, however, between all these and the French type of child care. The Roman, Spartan, chivalric, and British public-school type of education repressed a child's love for his parents – especially his mother – and displaced it on to the nation or the Church or the Empire, usually symbolized by the ruler. But the French type does not transfer devotion to something else, it simply sets it aside and substitutes individual comfort and pleasure, and a form of family coherence and affection which owes little to any wider community. The French apathy about politics is natural enough here. That this indifference is less than satisfactory even to the people who take it for granted can be seen in the way the stimulus of a common enemy brought out latent national feeling in the French during the war, and made a normally rhetorical patriotism into a force to be reckoned with.

After glancing at cultures that suppress the beginnings of love it is useful to look at another primitive society described by Margaret Mead in a book called *Growing up in New Guinea*. The Manus people have evolved a system of child-care which is almost the opposite of the French one in that a child's early years are care-free, surrounded by care and affection which progressively diminishes as the child grows. The marriage relationship is purely utilitarian – sex is a painful and shameful affair for the women, whose whole affection is therefore concentrated on their children. These are spoiled, petted and indulged to a degree beyond anything that even the most doting European parents would find allowable. The relationship between little girls and their fathers is particularly happy and close (as is often the case in cultures where the married sexual relationship is dutiful rather than personal and loving) and they quite normally sleep together. There is little differentiation between the sexes during childhood, and no obvious preparation is made for the assumption of adult duties. The children develop skills, but mainly for fun, and they run free, engaging in play that is exclusively physical in character, for there is no tradition of artistic effort among the Manus. This early spontaneity of behaviour and of affection is gradually and systematically suppressed as time goes on, both sexes conforming to a set of elaborate and rigid taboos that drain all adult energy into certain narrow channels aimed at material gain and security.

The Manus culture is only one of many that systematically suppress the development of love. It is especially interesting because it contradicts the conclusion, which might appear to follow from study of the other cultures mentioned, that early treatment is necessarily decisive for later life. Manus children are treated with all possible love and care, yet the adults are a community of deeply puritanical, repressed and exclusively materially minded people. The idea that early treatment permanently conditions the ability to love therefore needs to be qualified. It seems possible that it does so only negatively – that is, early affection is no guarantee of a loving adulthood, but early frustration of love is likely to lead to emotional inhibition later on. Yet even here we have to be careful. It might seem that harshness to children, an excess of discipline and the restriction of natural childish pleasures and activities would be the things that would adversely affect the child's emotional development. That the case is not so simple may be seen from the example of the type of education given to boys in Jewish culture of the eastern European type, which survives in modified forms in America, and is itself a direct descendant of traditional Jewish culture from the Biblical era onwards. The collection of studies from which I have quoted provides a description by Mark Zborowski of book-learning in the Jewish culture of the Shtetl, and the Jewish culture which he describes has been brought to life for many people by the musical, *Fiddler on the Roof*, which tells the story of a family in just such a poor but self-respecting Jewish community as Mark Zborowski observes.

This is a culture based on, and indeed encompassed by, the study of Scripture. For the orthodox Jew there is no other source of wisdom or learning and from the beginning a baby boy's future is thought of in terms of its study, so that the highest distinction his parents can hope for is that he will become a learned man, a scholar. He will be learned in the Torah only, for secular learning is trivial by comparison. Little girls are destined by hopeful mothers to marry scholars, and a girl who has the good fortune to marry a promising student may well go out to earn a living herself so that her husband may continue to study. Those men who are not good enough students to devote a lifetime to study will still give a certain amount of time to it every day, but especially on the Sabbath. The whole social hierarchy is based on the degree of attainment in the study of Scripture. Money is only valued because it gives leisure for this, and professions are valued in so far as they are related to scholarly attainment, so that manual labour is least regarded.

Study is the centre of a boy's life from the time he is old enough to learn his letters, between three and five years being the traditional age. At this early age a little boy was separated from his mother and taken to the Kheder, where he used to spend as much as twelve hours a day, every day except the Sabbath, often in a room much too small for the numerous pupils, shabby, uncomfortable and ill-lit. There were no aids to learning, though sweets were given on the first day to console the beginner. The boys learned the ancient text a word at a time, by rote, without at first understanding the meaning of what was read. The teacher was bored, and often harsh to the children since, oddly enough, his profession was despised and he only undertook it because he had failed to do better. Teaching the beginners was considered a contemptibly easy job, and indeed since nothing was required but forced repetition it certainly did not demand any great gifts in the teacher.

For a small and active child to spend days and months in a confined space, forced to attend to unutterably boring studies seems a recipe for stultification of the intellect and general stunting of personality. The French child's studies seem delightful by comparison. But, as Mark Zborowski remarks:

In this small, ill-ventilated room, packed with childish misery, are nourished the roots that will eventually blossom into a veritable passion for study, one in which zest is conspicuous. And from the uncomprehending rote repetition of syllables and words will develop an exuberant virtuosity in interpretation and endless analysis.

So the crushing boredom of the system did not crush the minds of these children. They were not damaged emotionally in any obvious way either, by this daily removal from home and mother, and subjection to harsh and arbitrary discipline. Jewish families have a deserved reputation for lasting affection, and relations between husband and wife are expected to be warm and strong. And the Jewish sense of community is a by-word, whether it be admired and envied, or regarded with suspicion and fear as proof of a conspiracy against other communities. This finding seems to contradict all the work of educationists who have laboured to deliver children from rote learning and set their minds free to explore and discover.

It is worth remembering in this context that the old methods of teaching music, by endless practising of scales and exercises, also, in many cases, developed into an exuberant virtuosity in interpretation and was even the prelude to the immense creativity of gifted composers. It is significant that the phrase used by this student of Jewish book culture should apply so obviously to the study of music, and for that matter to the other arts of painting and dancing, which have in many ages and cultures been studied first of all by means of tedious copying and unimaginative exercises. In the arts only the gifted individual is likely to transcend the routine and blossom into creative work, yet among those over-burdened Jewish infants there were few who did not grow up to find in study their deepest satisfaction, even though their attainment might be slight. The attitude of even the simplest is touchingly shown in the song in *Fiddler on the Roof* in which Tevye, the over-worked and always impoverished milkman who constantly mis-quotes 'The Good Book', dreams of being a rich man: beyond all the comfort and prestige that money might bring he longs for the greatest privilege that money can buy – leisure to study the Holy Book, and so, perhaps, in the end to gain the coveted 'seat by the Eastern wall' of the synagogue, where the learned men sit. Study brings social prestige, certainly, but the love of a poor and laborious people for Scripture is not merely a scramble for position. Rather, the position gained by study is an indication of the central importance of Scripture in the community's life. This is the clue to the reason why those oppressed children grew up to be spiritually and mentally exuberant, as well as generous in their family and community life. The child who is gifted in the arts can endure an incredible amount of boredom and restriction, and survive with his enthusiasm undimmed, because all the suffering is leading somewhere. There is a reaching out, however dimly understood, towards some vision, some goal that makes everything worthwhile. It is true that parental enouragement and even enforcement may be necessary to make the gifted child 'keep at it' and not give up, and this may also keep a less gifted child working, by the power of his parents', or perhaps his teacher's vision and drive. But it will only reach fruition if there is a real gift that makes the child capable, in the end, of seeing the vision for himself and assuming the struggle as his own responsibility. In the case of the child reared in the traditional Jewish pattern the vision is not dependent on personal gifts, though attainment obviously is. The vision is the thing that gives meaning to the life of the whole community. So the parents, and all the other grown-ups, keep this vision always before them and before the child. It is part of the air he breathes. Little though he may relish his early studies, he realizes gradually that this grinding effort is reaching out to something immensely important and wonderful, yet something which he is destined to share. It is his own personal hope towards which he is struggling, but this personal fulfilment is one with the fulfilment and glory of his people.

Here is a very marked form of that 'reaching further' quality of life that people seem to want, and whose deprivation impoverishes the human spirit. In the Balinese children it found an outlet in music and drama, but there was no overall purpose which was served, and the energy thus used was used up. There was nothing that could help to extend the spiritual liberation of artistic achievement to affect other areas of living and modify them. French culture appeared to channel all non-practical impulses into the pursuit of comfort and pleasure, and the traditional British tendency used to be (with the exception of the school of Anglo-Saxon 'je m'en fiche-ism') to give it room in romantic fantasies or in sport. It could also be almost totally suppressed, as among the Manus.

But there would seem, at first sight, to be no particular reason for saying that provision for this tendency to 'reach further' is necessary, or even a good thing. It seems to have been a basic assumption in most societies that it is not, and those who value it can bring little immediately convincing evidence in support. All the societies mentioned – and all the others I haven't mentioned which used an emotionally restrictive method of child-rearing – function very efficiently within their own terms, and achieve the aims of at least comparative stability and prosperity. There is also considerable evidence that societies exercising a consistently repressive type of child-care produce few delinquent children as compared with societies where there is more freedom. People alarmed by the criminal or at least 'anti-social' behaviour of the young often – reasonably – blame this state of affairs on the lack of traditional restrictive methods.

Before suggesting any conclusion about this it is necessary to notice that other factors are at work in these situations. There is not, as I have already noticed, a simple choice between the restrictive and the non-restrictive. The Manus children, after all, have freedom and a generous amount of parental love, yet grow up to conform to a severe moral code. 'Delinquency' does occur, but very seldom, and is regarded with deep horror. In Soviet Russia, once the early attempts to minimize parental influence in favour of community consciousness had been abandoned, the family was restored to a position of dignity and regarded as a primary influence in forming the Soviet citizen. The family, however, is not autonomous and is responsible to the community for its efforts to bring up good citizens. Its efforts must be unremitting and its goals according to correct socialist theory, but the methods to be used are by no means those of repression or harsh discipline. A Russian book on the training of Soviet children, quoted by Margaret Mead and Elena Calas in their study of 'child training ideals in a post-revolutionary context' demands that 'the atmosphere of the family must be one of comradeship, friendship, mutual help, industry, common political and cultural interests'. Parents are warned not to frighten children, either by physical punishment or by warnings of retribution. And freedom is emphasized: 'the child most of all needs freedom of action, . . . any oppression and interference in his life by adults can only destructively influence the flowering of his natural gifts.' This is balanced by warnings about the need for training in obedience and self-discipline, but nobody could bracket this approach with the régime imposed by Victorian parents. Yet juvenile delinquency has been, until recently, a minor problem in Soviet Russia, and this fact is often used by Soviet propagandists to point the contrast between healthy socialist youth and the degenerate young of a capitalist society. Also the comparatively recent increase in restlessness and nonconformity among Soviet youth is blamed on western influences, as well as on the failure of families to carry out zealously their task of socialist formation.

This attribution of blame is very much to the point. If what is required is a conformist society, of whatever type, what makes the difference is not harshness versus gentleness, or freedom versus restriction, but simply the unified or diverse nature of the influences brought to bear on the minds of children. In Soviet Russia the influences were all in the direction of socialist dedication and communal responsibility, they proposed and demanded conformity to one ideal pattern of Soviet citizenship in which family affection, friendship, personal achievement and cultural development all play a part, but all are subordinated to the creation and development of socialism, '... the communistic transformation of our motherland'. The pressures exerted are almost all moral and emotional pressures, but none the less effective for that, and all with the same intention. If the results have recently been less uniformly successful this is because other influences, from outside Russia but also generated within a society which no longer prevents all exchange of thought, have brought in question the absoluteness of the ideals proposed. The impact of new ideas on young people trained in a unified and conformist world is bound to be great, and the effect heady.

A similarly unified system of psychological pressures operate on Manus children as they grow older, and the Jewish child of the Shtetl was also protected from alien influences. But in America there are many cultural influences, and people who go to universities or even read a little are exposed to them (with results that the Jewish establishment deplores). But in spite of the American claim to emphasis on freedom, and especially freedom to achieve and advance by personal effort, the pressures for social conformity are very great, and most powerful in sections of society least exposed to influences other than the pressures of advertisers, emphasizing money, cleanliness, sexual prowess, fun, and so on.

The exploitation of the desire for gain is one of many

C

methods of producing a conforming society, of which some methods are comfortable and some not. What they have in common is a unified system of pressures leading to comparative stability and only a small number of non-conforming members. Whether conformity to the norm of a particular society is a sign of maturity or of de-humanization cannot, therefore, be decided by looking at the harshness or otherwise of the methods used to achieve conformity. Likewise the human value of a philosophy of child-care cannot be judged by whether or not the society in which it operates produces many or few 'delinquents'.

More useful as an indication of whether the 'reaching further' drive is humanly important is the nature of non-conformity in a given society. The type of delinquency that worries the Manus most is the sexual kind, because the stability of the society depends on the canalization of energy into the pursuit of gain. An unwed boy who seduces the girls upsets people, and risks rousing uncontrollable emotions, and society will go to great lengths to discourage the development of love between the sexes for the same reason. Margaret Mead quotes the case of Luwil and Molung, each engaged (by financial arrangement, in the usual way) to someone else. They were attracted to each other and slept together. After three days of this, Luwil's uncle, who had been away, was reported drowned, and the village mourned, and looked around for the culprit, for all disasters are held to be due to someone's sin. Molung and Luwil held themselves responsible, even when it was found that the lost man was safe. Afraid to confess, they fled to another village where Luwil had a friend. When his own village realized what had happened a marriage was quickly patched up, to prevent the sin from bringing more disasters, but Margaret Mead emphasizes that this only happened because this couple had a friend to go to. Normally, an offending couple would have nowhere to go, would be obliged to confess, and would be separated, for no Manus household would shelter such a couple, lest the spirits punish the inmates. Significantly, Margaret Mead notes that Luwil and Molung 'were one of the rare cases where husband and wife got on fairly happily together, perhaps because the affair began by their own choice'. Such marriages are discouraged because real love might grow in them and threaten the stability of a society based on property, which is mainly apportioned by the financial arrangement called marriage. This attitude was also prevalent in the upper classes in England in the late eighteenth and early nineteenth centuries, and wayward emotion was correspondingly outlawed as 'illbred'; the higher the social position the less was there room for love in marriage, for it upset the intricate financial balancing acts involved.

In Soviet society the types of non-conformity that seem to threaten society are more likely to be the pursuit of unusual or obscure art forms, open criticism of the establishment, or types of music and dancing that release strong emotion of a kind that cannot be directed to the good of the state. Any of these bring into question the absoluteness of the correct socialist ideal. In the same way, long hair, pacifism and an unwillingness to work are types of non-conformity that upset Americans whose society is based on a mythologized Founding Fathers ideal which includes a stereotyped notion of maleness, a 'defence of freedom' militancy and above all an emphasis on getting on by one's own efforts.

All these types of non-conformity are in some way or other protests against what is felt as an unjustified restriction of the human spirit. I say 'unjustified' because restriction can be accepted when the purpose of it is worthwhile, as I indicated in the case of Jewish methods of education. But there are other forms of non-conformity that bear a very different interpretation, and these are the kind we most frequently find in our own society, even though others (the 'long-haired and irresponsible' variety) may get much more attention from a nervous establishment.

European and American societies think they want children to learn to love. And in efforts to bring this about we release some of the pressures that might produce conformity. Conformity is very supporting, a feeling of belonging keeps people going through hardship and even under great injustice, both social and economic. But the type of school education that is more and more usual in the west is *not* designed to apply unified pressure to produce a certain ideal. It has abandoned old certainties and largely failed to offer alternative goals. This, plus a general uncertainty about whether moral norms matter, means that the hand of society's moral preconceptions is much less felt, and with the removal of its weight goes the removal of its support. But the child still needs support, and the only people who can now give it are the parents. What happens when, often enough, they cannot give it? The child has no clear sense of identity, no clear moral direction, nothing to aim at. Juvenile delinquency, in its most common form, is the result of the removal of unified social pressures plus the failure of parental influence. The Victorian pauper child, neglected and abandoned by his parents, might easily turn criminal and find in the underworld a consistent moral pattern. But given a 'chance' in a bleak and overcrowded orphanage, or by individual charity, he could, and often did, grow up law-abiding and even content, because the whole force of society's influence demanded certain clear moral standards from him. A similar child nowadays lacks this support, and has a correspondingly greater difficulty in orientating himself successfully among his fellows. It is interesting that nowadays efforts to help such children usually consist in giving them parent-substitutes of some kind in the hope that they will discover in them the support that will enable them to 'find their feet' and develop properly. The assumption is that *love* is what matters, with reasonable social adaptation as a consequence. In cases where the child is so disturbed that he cannot form a normal relationship the same goal is pursued with the specialized help of a psychiatrist. His job is not to suppress anti-social behaviour but to discover the emotional lack that causes it, and help the child to recognize his own feelings, accept them, and therefore begin to be able to adjust to other people.

He is, in fact, doing the opposite of what most societies would consider desirable. Instead of bringing pressure to bear to make the child conform he tries to help to release pressures and let him discover his own individuality, but in a protective and supporting setting where he need not fear the strength of his own feelings. Sometimes it works, and the child eventually becomes 'normal' with the normal chances of making satisfactory personal relationships. Sometimes it doesn't work, and the child never really finds his place in society.

On the face of it, the heavy pressure towards conformity seems kinder as well as more orderly. The chances of reasonable contentment, if not of great happiness, seem to be greater that way. Certainly it is no wonder that most societies throughout history have looked with suspicion, derision, or active disapproval, on methods of education aimed at developing individual freedom and the ability to love.

Our own society seems to have embarked on the perilous course of allowing freedom and love, but in a rather vague and hopeful way. This is partly deliberate and influenced by modern psychology, but the release of pressures is mainly unintentional, and is due to the multiplicity of influences that make a clear overall moral influence impossible. What no culture has tried yet is a unified educational influence deliberately designed both to make love and freedom possible and to provide the supporting framework that can allow this to go on without social disaster.

II

SEXUAL LOVE: THE RESTRICTION OF SEX

IN the West the tendency is to regard sexual love as the most important and frequent kind of love. There is no way of measuring the degree of love in any relationship – between parents and children, siblings, friends, teachers and pupil and so on – in order to count how many loving relationships of each kind there might be, and nobody agrees on a definition of love anyway, while its constant association with sex above all has made the whole question even more ambiguous. For instance there is a clear shift in meaning between the statements 'he made love to her', and 'she loves her child'. The two meanings are constantly used, but no one bothers to ask how the same word can possibly be the correct one in both cases, when everyone who uses the first knows that it may refer to a relationship in which there is no trace of love, in the second sense. One way out is to say that there is no 'real' love in the second case either, but in both cases merely a kind of appetite. (Yet the fact that we can deny the existence of love in one or both cases shows that a meaning is attached to the word which goes beyond either use.) An attractive conclusion is that there is no such thing as love, but the word is used to disguise the cowardly flight from brutal reality.

This was Nietzsche's view. Love was the thing he most feared; it was the enemy of achievement and power and all he admired. This view is more common than might be supposed. Nietzsche spoke for many and he spoke more truly than some who uphold love as the panacea for a sick society and a substitute for moral law. He knew that just as love would be, for him, an abdication of the ambition to stand alone, so it has always threatened to undermine human political achievement. In Wagner's *Ring* Valhalla crumbles into the flames because the rule of the old gods, based on an impersonal justice overriding all human emotion, is undermined by Brunnhilde's decision to defy the law and help the fugitive Sieglinde in her plight. From that act of compassionate disobedience flows the chain of events that finally destroys the whole system, heroes and all. This myth expresses very clearly why any system of human power is afraid of love and tries to suppress, restrict, divert or dilute it.

In order to begin to clarify the relation between sex and love the next two chapters are both concerned with love in a sexual context, but I have divided the subject into two. This chapter is mainly about the restriction of sex, the next about the glorification or cultivation of sex, and how love fares in each case. The tentative definition of love that I gave in the last chapter should take on a sharper outline from the use of the word in these contexts.

There will inevitably be a good deal of overlapping in the subject matter between these two chapters and the first, since sexual customs and reactions grow directly out of childhood patterns of care and behaviour, as the last chapter indicated.

It is sometimes assumed that the restriction of sex is exclusive to the Christian culture (possibly the Jewish one too) and this dismal state is contrasted with the happy freedom of primitive and 'pagan' peoples nowadays, and of our remote ancestors. But even the most apparently uninhibited communities turn out on closer inspection to have *some* rigid restrictions, and there is no correlation whatever between primitiveness and sexual freedom. As the last chapter indicated, among the Manus of New Guinea sex was degraded and closely controlled in a way that would delight the heart of any puritan or an early Father of the Church. It has become fashionable to compare the frank sexuality of Hindu art with the guilt-ridden sex life of Christian Europe, and it is forgotten that Hindu erotic art is religious in meaning and has nothing to say about the rules and prohibitions governing day-to-day relationships between the sexes. Sexual relations for Hindus were and are (apart from other considerations) contained within a strictly controlled caste system, that cuts off one group of people totally from another. Sexual 'freedom' across these lines was liable to result in death or mutilation. In the West, the fact of ritual prostitution in the ancient Greek shrines of Aphrodite tells us nothing about the sexual behaviour of Hellenic families of the time. A recent handbook on Yoga designed for an English and American public makes it tactfully but unambiguously clear that sex is something the man mature in meditation will learn to do without. Ghandi, in later life, had a horror of sex as deep as any Christian hermit's, and in fact on one occasion subjected his chastity to the same test that was once reputedly practised by Christian spiritual athletes – that of sleeping in the same bed with a young girl. Buddhism, also, much more explicitly than Christianity, regards the rejection of sex and of human affection as necessary to the attainment of freedom.

All of this is not to deny that the Christian tradition has a great deal to do with the guilt about sex that still plagues our culture, but even the brief references just given should dispel the idea that the Christian culture has been unique in its distrust of sex.

The cultivation of sexual repulsion is a usual way of restricting sex. Attitudes of repulsion and guilt are *learned*. We are so used to our own set of repulsions that we tend to think of them as 'natural', and people who don't have them as immoral or at least uncivilized, but there is no such thing as a 'natural' repulsion. The western child learns to be disgusted by his own excrement. Children of other cultures often have no such prejudice. It is even fairly recent in our own culture.

These learned repulsions are very deeply rooted. Our own society has a long tradition of repulsive reactions to certain types of sexual behaviour, and when they are in operation they appear to be as absolute and as basic as the notions of sin and virtue themselves. The following quotation refers to a guilt about pre-marital sex, a type which has been (and still to a great extent is) prevalent in our own society, but the same type of reaction may however be found in any kind of society where sexual prohibitions are of the 'taboo' type, that is, prohibitions inculcated at a sub-rational level and producing a strong emotional reaction of repulsion, or of guilt in those who transgress. George Moore's *Esther Waters* is a very perceptive study of a girl with sensitive moral responses. The conflict between her reason and natural affection, and her sub-rational guilt, is apparent here. Esther, in love with William, and rather hazy with harvest beer and a warm evening among the hay-stacks, has allowed his urgent desire to overcome her principles. Afterwards, she will not speak to him and avoids him for days:

> She had not willed to give herself; he had taken advantage of her in a moment of weakness. This was how she understood her sin; and if her heart sometimes softened, and an insidious thought whispered that it did not matter since they were going to be married, an instinct forced her to act in contradiction to her desire. She felt that she could only win his respect by refusing forgiveness for a long while. The religion in which her soul moved and lived – the sternest Protestantism – strengthened and reinforced the original convictions and prejudices of her race, and the natural shame which she had at first felt almost disappeared in the violence of her virtue. She even ceased to fear discovery. What did it matter who knew, since she knew? And on her knees at night she opened her heart to God. Christ looked down, and He seemed stern and unforgiving.

Hers was the unpardonable sin, the sin which her race had elected to fight against. She lay down heavy and sullen at heart. Her Christ was the Christ of her forefathers; and He had not forgiven, because she could not forgive herself.

George Moore sums it up admirably in the phrase 'the sin which her race had elected to fight against'. Other serious prohibitions there may be, but those actions to which people are taught to react with immediate repulsion are the ones that determine and indicate the goals of a culture. Religion defines and enforces such repulsions, with supernatural dread of rejection, and also with spiritual rewards for virtue, because the institutions and aims which are protected in this way are the ones on which tribal or national survival depends. Changed values mean a changed culture: the people may survive but the culture does not, if its 'shape' is radically altered by the failure of its taboos and the growth of others. Therefore it sprouts whatever system of sub-rational repulsions is necessary to preserve them, and its religion – its mythological self-definition – expounds and enforces these.

The smaller, more homogeneous societies that anthropologists have studied show a unified system with few variations in the pattern of behaviour laid down by custom, and exceptions show up sharply as exceptions rather than as permissible variations. Noticing the way they control sex should make it easier to discover the directions of the more complex patterns of European culture, formed by multiple influences and having a variety of motivations operating within one society.

The Manus, already referred to, are an example that springs to mind because their particular version of sexual restraints is so extreme. It is also strikingly like the combination of sexual puritanism and emphasis on material things that characterized the rise of capitalism, whose Protestantism provided an Old-Testament-type justification of the obsession with material possessions, which were seen as a sign of God's approval of the virtuous man. Both kinds of society have a type of sexual repression that is fairly straightforward and its reasons not hard to uncover. It will help to look at this type of control before examining more exotic and deeply-hidden reasons.

The Manus were a people living in unpropitious conditions, so that the efforts of men and women had to be focused on work, and idleness was regarded as shameful. They made few beautiful things themselves, but confined their efforts to making what was required for a living. Their devotion to work was reinforced by their religion, which was mainly a belief in the power of the dead to punish descendants who do not put their backs into essential enterprises. The nineteenth-century European and American work-worship showed a similar reinforcement not by ghosts but by a religious-type duty to follow in father's (or grandfather's) footsteps, go into the family business, get a good job or make good money. Behind this again was the God whose likes and dislikes bore such a strong resemblance to those of Father.

This religious devotion to work as a good in itself, and the importance of its results in material possessions as a measure of the person's social status was, not surprisingly, accompanied by a very business-like attitude to marriage. What mattered was the exchange of property that took place between the families when a marriage was arranged, and the wishes of the couple were not considered. An arranged marriage can be very happy, and sexually contented, but if it is the personal relationship between husband and wife becomes very important to them, and they have correspondingly less interest in other things. Work no longer seems supremely virtuous, material possessions may come to be regarded as merely the necessary and pleasant setting for the relationship. In a society whose existence depends on constant effort such a dilution of zeal for gain is inadmissible, and among Manus peoples it was prevented with great thoroughness, and almost complete success, by a view of life that equated sex with excretion, and regarded both as inherently degrading and shameful. Women were taught to regard their husband's sexual demands as a humiliation they were obliged to undergo, and from which they could expect only discomfort. The discomfort was made almost inevitable by a taboo on any kind of sexual fore-play, so that the act of intercourse between husband and wife was a form of routine rape. A woman whom it was customary, indeed required, to treat in this fashion could not in the nature of things be an object of respect, let alone affection. In her child-bearing days the wife was scolded, despised and valued only for her ability to work. But it is interesting that in middle life, when child-bearing was over, married couples became much more friendly and even enjoyed each other's company. This is not unusual in our own society even now when the sexual rivalry – to some extent disguised by a vestigial romanticism – of earlier years gives way to a more companionable relationship, always provided the marriage lasts that long. But it used to be considerably more common, in Protestant cultures in Europe and New England, where young women were regarded with wary suspicion, if not of their personal character, at least of their inevitable sexual vulnerability and therefore of their character as both dangerous and somehow sacred. They had to prove their virtue and respectability by submissiveness, frequent child-bearing, and hard work, whereas an older woman had a more assured position, more respect from her husband and others, and in her turn kept the young women in their place.

Among the Manus, adultery was regarded with strong aversion, since it upset the careful marital finances. Women, as the more 'bodily' sex, were more heavily penalized for sexual sin, and the ghosts of dead husbands were supposed to be especially angry at them. Male adultery was also strictly forbidden within the tribe, but no angry ghosts protested if a group of men on a war expedition captured a woman and used her as a prostitute. Young men, sexually deprived while waiting for marriage, would take an unfortunate captive to some remote place, where a group of these extremely potent but repressed males could revenge themselves on one helpless woman for the unadmitted anger and shame they were forced to suffer in their sexual lives at home. The traditional attitude of respectable and prosperous western society to servant-girls or any women of 'the lower classes' used to be remarkably similar. In both cases the reason (obscured by the fact that such taboos act at a sub-rational level) seems to be that the encouragement of sexual satisfaction in marriage would undermine the drive to material gain and the structure of a society based on this, but male sexuality exercised on women with no social and financial status does not threaten the social arrangements whereby property is controlled and stabilized and increased, therefore no taboo operates here. Boys from well-to-do families in England, like medieval pages, learned to despise girls, to be embarrassed by their mothers' and sisters' visits to school, and to find sexual experience with other boys or with lower-class girls. This does not affect property. Women, on the other hand, could not be allowed sex on the side because this would remove them from the home, where they are required to be for the sake of social continuity and control.

Another Manus compensating arrangement was that whereby a man was expected to be on terms of sexual intimacy, short of intercourse, with a female cousin, while the human closeness and tenderness which we associate with marriage but which was denied to him there, was allowed to exist between brother and sister. This is an unusually thorough and explicit method of making sure that there is never any whole (mental–spiritual–physical) relationship between a man and woman, but the situation is not allowed to become quite unbearable, as it might be if all tenderness between man and woman, and all sexual play and pleasure, were entirely ruled out.

In the west, the arrangements for preventing a full relationship in marriage were, even at the height of the Puritan ethic, much less explicit and therefore less successful. Sex in marriage might be furtive, shameful and – for the woman – degrading and possibly painful, but it was still possible for a relationship of mutual respect and affection to grow up. In some marriages sex was satisfactory and pleasurable, in spite of everything, but often the sexual aspect of life was regarded as a regrettable necessity which the considerate husband would inflict on his wife only because he needed to. The wife would accept it with patience because she recognized the need, and because both wanted children. It need not and did not interfere with the important things of life – home and children and friends, enjoyed and worked at together, in a relationship that was increasingly satisfactory to both, and which middle age made easier by lessening the power of the potentially disruptive sexual drive.

But in marriages where such affection could not find a way round the sub-rational taboos, something similar to the Manus arrangements did occur in western society and still does, though it is not a universal and socially recognized phenomenon. At a party, for instance, it is not uncommon for a married man to spend the evening flirting openly with a friend's wife, or perhaps with a single woman who is of mature age but still attractive, and his wife will not mind – or at any rate will do well to conceal the fact if she does. Such a man will not normally choose a young girl as his flirting partner because this would be too approximate to adultery; if he did do so his wife would have real grounds for objecting, and his friends would disapprove. The allowed flirtation, which is often of long standing, is recognized by all and may include a certain amount of hearty physical endearment such as patting, kissing, and slapping of bottoms. It seems to be similar to the Manus permission of sexual play between cross-cousins, which is not allowed with other women, or in marriage. It seems possible that this happens in marriages in which sex is rapid and unsatisfactory for the woman, either because of the wife's prudery or frigidity, or the husband's secret scorn of women and equation of tenderness with weakness. The comparison is certainly suggestive, and may perhaps be tested by the reader's own knowledge of individuals exhibiting this kind of behaviour.

The role of the feminine confidant has been important in western society. The completely un-physical but deep and even passionate relationship between certain sensitive and highly cultured men and women is part of our literary and artistic background, and it does seem to be associated with an aversion to sex as degrading. Swift had his Stella, and his feelings of disgust about sex are apparent in his writings. Kirkegaard loved Regina Olsen until a marriage became a real possibility. Tschaikovsky could not make anything of his marriage but found his relationship, purely by letter, with Madame von Meik extremely satisfying. Possibly he was homosexual, but this also can occur because of a revulsion against normal sex, and so therefore against women, and this, too, happened in Manus society. Homosexual relationships, however, are frowned on especially if there is any real love involved, because this also is a threat to marriage and therefore to the economic stability of society.

One other example of this type of compensation for deprivation in marriage is peculiar to English society. The English Nanny could and did become the real 'mother' of lonely children whose biological mother was too inhibited to indulge in physical endearment or comfort. She was often the confidant of the schoolboy and the adult, giving a warm affection and support, and a feminine influence both earthy and strong yet uncontaminated by sexual associations. This could continue after marriage, and many a middle-aged stockbroker wept at the grave of his nurse more bitterly than at those of father, mother or wife.

The other type of tender relationship permitted among the Manus was that between parents and small children, and especially between father and daughter. Women deprived of affection and status as wives naturally cling to their children and feel intensely about them. Among the Manus the mother soon lost her influence over the children, who learned to make constant demands and to expect total obedience. The boys, especially, soon learned the role of women as that despised but necessary economic convenience, a wife. But while they were little the mother made the most of their weakness and need. In our society it is still common for unsatisfied wives to cling to their children and demand from them the emotional satisfaction they cannot find in marriage. But whereas among the Manus strict custom withdrew the children from her influence fairly soon, in the west there is no control over a mother's desire to keep her children little and needy except her own conscience, or the children's strength of character. Social disapproval exists, but it is not explicit enough to enforce conformity by pressure of custom, the threat of the stigma of social ostracism, or religious sanctions. Possessiveness has not been conventionally classed either as a sin or as a social solecism.

The father–daughter relationship, however, provides an even closer parallel. The father in both types of Puritanism may licitly make a close friend of his small daughter, play with her, caress her, and indulge her. The sternest of Victorian fathers was known to unbend to a small girl in a frilled pinafore and ringlets, who would sit on his knee and stroke his face and kiss him – conduct he would not welcome from his wife, unless he managed to think of her also as a child, and therefore in some way unsexed. In his famous portrait of Dora, David Copperfield's 'child-wife', Dickens was evoking a recognized ideal – the girl-wife who was so 'innocent' and ignorant that she could scarcely be regarded as sexually a woman. By making her emotionally a little girl, a man trained to regard sex as degrading could manage to develop a real desire for his wife-to-be, or young wife, without recognizing that, like the Manus father, his delight in the 'little girl' was in fact sexual in character. Lewis Carroll loved being with little girls, and photographing them. He was probably not a pervert, but an ordinary man like thousands of others who found in the delicate (but un-sexual) femininity of a child an acceptable substitute for the relationship with a grown-up woman which would inevitably be spoiled by her sexual nature.

Dickens's Dora has a miscarriage and dies soon after; in other words the child-wife can never be the mature woman. Middle-class wives who demonstrated their adulthood by conceiving concealed their pregnancy as if it were a revolting illness, and never referred to it directly. The presence of an actual baby, however, managed somehow to confer on the mother a sort of sympathetic childhood, and an aura of inviolability.

This particular result, at least, of sexual control by disgust – the cultivation of infantile characteristics in a grown woman – was avoided by the Manus. Taboos descended upon the girl as she grew up, and gradually confined her to the society of women and to her future as a wife in a depressed but resigned maturity. In this condition she could, if she had the brains, compensate for lack of affection from her husband, and loss of her growing children, by gaining prestige and power as a business woman. The 'career woman' of western society is sometimes a by-product of sexual control by repulsion. Married women may find satisfaction that way, but some elect to avoid degradation and subservience by remaining unmarried and getting satisfaction in a career. This would not have happened among the Manus, where every woman married, but the impulse has the same root. In many – by no means all – cases the self assertion of a 'career woman' of this type is not against sex but against a feminine role based on the repulsion from sex, which involves the social 'punishment' of women who are *the* sexual beings. Even though her own sex life may be satisfactory, such a woman needs to reject the classification of herself as female in this sense that has become traditional.

Religious virginity has been a part of many cultures, and dedicated men and women had an honoured place in many ancient religions. This did not necessarily imply any disgust with sex, however. In some cases the virgins were regarded as the property of the god, and therefore to seduce one was to commit adultery. (The Hebrew classification of adultery with theft, as an offence against property, was normal among the ancient cultures of the Middle East.)

The exaltation of virginity as actually possessing some kind of holiness which is not available to the married is not a peculiarly Christian notion. In Bali the virgins, and women past child-bearing, are described as 'seeking Heaven', and are given a role in religious ritual which is denied to married women of child-bearing age. The Balinese do not regard sex as repulsive, but virginity, or widowhood, releases certain kinds of spiritual energy which are appropriate to worship. The same idea seems to be present in Buddhism, since monastic life does not imply a revulsion from sex but a concentration of energy on the pursuit of spiritual freedom. Love was to be withdrawn from created things in order to reach beyond them, to the All from which they emerged but beside which they were unreal. This idea, common to mystics of many religions, is only incidentally related to the rejection of sex and sexual love. What matters to mystics is the positive good which is pursued, not what is discarded on the way. When he was alive the Buddha seems to have envisaged his Way as one for ordinary people and it was only gradually that it became apparent that complete following of the Way required something like a monastic life. The rejection of sex as evil proves, in general, to be less than helpful to true mystical awareness, since such revulsion implies a preoccupation with sex, and what the mystic needs is not revulsion but freedom and peace. G. Rattray Taylor in *Sex in History* attacks the false Christian attitudes to sex, and points out that the proliferation of detailed studies of sexual sins and misconduct in medieval penitentiaries, and works on the spiritual life, shows an obsession with the subject which is precisely the opposite of the detachment from too absorbing emotion which is recommended by mystics of many faiths or none. Professor Rattray Taylor's book is too undiscriminating in its use of sources, too careless about checking the accuracy of his facts by relevant modern research, and in particular too prone to taking facts out of context and drawing conclusions to fit his own chosen theory to make it possible to take the work seriously. (It is an excellent and informed historical romp, however, as long as one doesn't expect to discover in it anything so complex as real roots of human sexual behaviour.) But it must be admitted that the temptation for any non-Christian writer to jump to the conclusions that he wanted to reach must have been immense, because there is no doubt that Christianity has produced, at various periods, a fantastic crop of hideous sexual obsessions and aberrations. Yet even anti-Christian historians usually admit that the attitude to life attributed to Jesus of Nazareth in the four Gospels shows no sign of this anti-sexual madness. There is little mention of sex, though traditional sexual imagery is common. Marital faithfulness is enjoined, lustful imaginations condemned, virginity 'for the Kingdom' presented as holy but not *de rigueur*. Women are treated with love and respect and sexual sinners with understanding. What happened to make so great a change among the later followers of Jesus?

Paul of Tarsus is usually blamed for the shift in Christian feeling, at least by people who have not studied his thought but merely picked out a few (poorly translated) texts. But even if he had been the sex-obsessed anti-feminist that his enemies depict he could not have swung the whole, growing Christian tradition into a path so unlike that of its early decades unless there had been a strong predisposition that way in the young communities. There certainly was such a tendency, and the much maligned Paul spent a good deal of energy combating it, or trying at least to modify its excesses to a point where behaviour could be compatible with the emerging theology of the new life.

In a book which must necessarily range over wide areas of human experience, it would be foolish to try to explain fully why the Christian ethic became so obsessed with sexuality. This much can be said: the Christian teaching about the new life in Christ, into which the believer entered by faith but which would be fully established when 'the world and the flesh' (meaning all that is unredeemed and blind in human nature) would be overcome, did lend itself to an interpretation that emphasized the rejection of physical experience and pleasure, even of beauty, and the exaltation of the spiritual, here meaning non-physical. But even if this had been a valid interpretation of the Gospel message (and modern research shows that it is not) it would not account for the obsessive quality of the anti-sex theme. Buddhism in several of its forms emphasizes the Great Renunciation and prescribes an extremely frugal and disciplined life, and the best of the early Christian monks and ascetics did the same. But the lunatic fringe of Christian asceticism rivals the excesses of some Hindu sects, and it had a hold on the popular mind, so that stories of feats of self-torture were preserved with admiration by people themselves wholly disinclined for anything of the kind. These excesses were, during the early centuries and the 'dark ages', confined to a small number, but it was in fact a popular movement in the sense that it was somehow emotionally meaningful to the millions whose own sexual behaviour was ruled by tradition, local custom, ordinary lust and ordinary love. Yet towards the end of the Middle Ages even ordinary people seemed to be seized with this madness, and processions of flagellants with bleeding backs could be seen passing through the streets of medieval cities. In Spain and Italy it continued into the high Renaissance and even the eighteenth century and in Mexico it is still to be found. A movement of feeling so widespread and so deep-rooted that it can, in some people and at certain times, sweep aside all ordinary human dislike of pain, all normal family affection as well as everyday sensuality, cannot be simply due to some doctrine intellectually accepted, and indeed the official teaching of the Church discouraged such excesses both in theory and practice, while its official creed continued (rather unconvincingly in the circumstances), to state the goodness of creation, the dignity of marriage and the holiness of the human body that was destined to be finally transformed in Christ. But few churchmen applied this doctrine. The full pressure of 'the spirit of the age' was against them; it may help to show how powerful this pressure *against* the orthodox teaching was if we realize something not often mentioned, that the Catharist heretics, whose doctrine explicitly rejected the body as evil and sex as invariably sinful, were so numerous that in the thirteenth century they threatened to outnumber the Catholics. So the fervent (both heretic and orthodox) continued their castigation of sex and women, while other churchmen, rendered cynical by such a spectacle, drifted to those extremes of debauchery and venality that have made the late medieval Church a scandal to all ages since.

Only a mind as fantastic as those of the inquisitors themselves could seriously maintain (as has been done) that this anti-sex drive was deliberately cultivated in an attempt by the Church to retain its power over sinful people afraid of hell and clinging to the Church's power of absolution. There is not a shred of evidence to support such an idea, and considerable evidence (as even Shaw realized) for the sincerity of the sex-obsessed clerics. In any case it is not as simple as that. A madness seized on Europe for centuries, and a less prejudiced look at the situation shows that Church officials were as much victims of this madness as anyone else. The fact that they tried to give it explicit justification and to codify it in manuals for confessors, in works on witchcraft and so on, is merely the difference that always exists between the more or less inarticulate men who simply feel and react to the currents of popular emotion, and the men who recognize, explain and justify such feelings in words and so make the situation explicit for all.

But the fact that some people do put emotions into words is very important in understanding the development of characteristic styles in various cultures. The emotional reactions of the inarticulate do not antedate the verbalization. Emotion finds its full existence and power in its definition by the lips of people able to express what they know. The way it is expressed naturally depends on the notions of the nature of human life in which men have been educated. If the men concerned are Christians, the trend of thought takes shape in terms of a Christian kind of 'language', and the language of theology itself is modified in the process. This complicated interaction of inarticulate desires and fears exploding into words, the particular words giving channels to the emotions and the words themselves being changed by this process, is the process of cultural change and development.

One example of how this works, which is basic to the anti-sex theme in Europe, is the alteration of the word translated as 'flesh' in many English versions of the new Testament. In Paul's writing, derived from the Jewish usage, the word means the state of mortal man, subject to illness and fear and sin, liable to be deceived and pushed around by half-understood emotion. In particular there is a sense that 'the flesh' is vulnerable, man has no security and will die. Paul takes this concept further than his ancestors and sees in 'the flesh' the state from which man is freed by Christ, against which, therefore, he is struggling. It is in this sense that Paul regards 'the flesh' as the enemy, and since man is a physical being, bodily feelings and desires and ailments are obvious targets for criticism, when they are 'fleshly' and impede the transformation of the whole man. But 'the flesh' is not equated with the body, nor is the body evil, or its acts defiling or unworthy in themselves. On the contrary, the sex act in ordinary human marriage is used as a symbol of Christ's union with his people, and over-ascetic converts are reminded that ill-treating the body can actually be a form of indulgence of 'the flesh'.

This use of the word 'flesh' was lost, because doctrines that polarized body and soul, the material and the spiritual, were superimposed on the earlier teaching. 'The flesh' became synonymous with 'the body' as the material principle opposed to the spirit. So we get the now familiar idea of 'the soul' which is good, enclosed in the corrupt and perishable body. This body is regarded as evil; in certain heretical sects it is actually the creation of the evil Power which is opposed to God. If in the orthodox Christian tradition the body is held to be created by God, it is regarded as so corrupted that attitudes to it are much the same in both cases. The word 'flesh' comes to mean not only 'the body' but especially 'the sinful body' and its sins are overwhelmingly sexual.

This strange alteration in meaning 'justifies' as well as expresses the preoccupation with sexual sin, the suspicion and humiliation of women (who had been well respected in the early Church) and the hysterical exaltation of virginity as a value in itself. The restriction of sexual love by a religious system could hardly have been more thorough than it was during the Middle Ages. It was much more obsessive than during the earlier period of the desert Fathers, when popular attitudes were still influenced by the surviving pagan cultures. By the Middle Ages the barbarians had wiped out most of that earlier culture, and the passage of time had allowed Christian ideas, but by then in the altered form mentioned above, to take their place in ethical thinking, and at the root of unconscious repulsions.

Such vague phrases as the 'medieval mind' or 'western culture' may be merely advertising slogans, but they can have a real validity when we are trying to show what were the conscious assumptions, myths, uses of language, and so on, by which a particular culture understood itself and therefore tried to regulate its behaviour. But it is misleading if it is supposed that such descriptions exhaust the reality of the human situation to which they refer. If, for instance, the pattern of sexual repulsions of the fourteenth-century European had been the sum of the individual's sexual feelings and behaviour, his grandsons and great-grandsons would have felt and behaved in the same way, since they would be conditioned by a unified set of influences. In fact no individual is wholly determined by the approved pattern of feeling and behaviour in his culture, even if he strives to be completely conforming. He has feelings he does not fully understand, however intelligent and perceptive he may be, and these operate 'underground'. When these feelings are not too obviously opposed to the current cultural prejudices, they can generally be accommodated within the conscious pattern of the culture, which will make efforts to fit them in. Thus the natural desire of a man to make love to his wife, simply because he is fond of her, is not readily explained in terms of a doctrine that regards sexual desire as inevitably corrupt and justified (if at all) only by the desire for offspring. But intercourse without the explicit desire for offspring could escape sinfulness, in the opinion of some moralists at least, if it was done to avoid the greater evil of adultery and was the 'payment of the (marriage) debt'. It seems that some theologians, probably including St Thomas Aquinas (but he is contradictory and elusive on the subject) thought that 'paying the debt' could be made to include intercourse whose sole motive was mutual love. In this way what we might regard as the normal and most laudable motive for marital intercourse did get in, by the back door. By getting in, it gradually modified established sexual attitudes.

But sometimes human feelings cannot be accommodated within the current range of acceptable behaviour and in this case they are labelled as 'sin' or something similar. But if they are strong and important to a large number this simply won't do, at any rate over a long period, because there are limits to the amount of procrustean trimming that human nature will put up with. In such cases you get a cultural revolution, rather than evolution, but even so the emerging culture will, for some time, understand itself in similar terms to that which it supersedes.

The Renaissance was such a cultural revolution. Suppressed aspects of human experience clamoured to become a recognized part of the pattern of human living. And among the most important of the human experiences that demanded recognition was sexual love. For at this period for the first time the word 'love' in reference to relations between the sexes is beginning to be used in something like the way we use it now, and as it had not been used since St Paul used it in his few references to married love.

One man stood at the meeting point of the two cultures, or rather at the point where they clashed and the old one fell in ruins, though its outlines succeeded in imposing their form on the concepts of the new age. Shakespeare's varying attitudes to sexual love make a good transition to the study, in the next chapter, of the cultivation of sex.

One aspect of Shakespeare's sexual doctrine is a pre-occupation with virginity, and in this he shares the attitude of medieval Europe. Virginity is not simply regarded as honour-able, and to be guarded, but as a focus for sexually coloured imaginings. It is almost impossible to mention the fact that a girl is a virgin without producing a reaction of almost super-stitious reverence, of cynical suspicion or of bawdy suggestion. Lucio, in *Measure for Measure*, is a light-hearted lecher with no greater respect for truth than women, but speaking to the would-be novice Isabella he protests at her doubt of his truthfulness, for although he is used

> . . . to jest,
> Tongue, far from heart,

with maidens (the implication being that these maids are only precariously in that condition) he does not

> play with all Virgins so:
> I hold you as a thing enskie'd and sainted;
> By your renouncement, an imortall spirit;
> And to be talk'd with in sincerity,
> As with a Saint.

This reverence for the fact of virginity is so deep-rooted that it contradicts all the man's (and the age's) natural attitude of easy cynicism about women. This reverence is not related to any positive virtue in Isabella – Lucio has never met her before.

But in his mind the physical fact of virginity confers on her a numinous power, over himself – to make him speak with unaccustomed truthfulness – and over Angelo with whom he asks her to plead for her brother's life:

> Goe to Lord Angelo,
> And let him learne to know, when Maidens sue,
> Men give like gods; but when they weep and kneele,
> All their petitions are as freely theirs
> As they themselves would owe them.

Virginity and integrity are used as virtually synonymous. 'Honour' for a girl means her virginity. The physical fact of virginity is equated with personal value, and the loss of virginity, even when it is forced, is a destruction of some personal value. Virginity once lost, efforts at virtue are held to be useless. Thus in *Pericles*, Boult, fed up with Marina's tight hold on her 'Virgin knot', and her refusal therefore to entertain customers, decides that, 'Faith, I must ravish her, or she'll disfurnish us of all our cavalereea'. It is assumed that once she has been ravished she will give no further trouble, since her 'virtue' will be gone for good. 'Crack the glass of her virginitie, and make the rest malliable', says the Bawd.

This can apply even to the loss of virginity in marriage. In speaking of his boyhood friendship with Leontes, Polixenes in *The Winter's Tale* claims that

> we knew not
> The Doctrine of ill-doing, nor dream'd
> That any did. Had we pursu'd that life,
> And our weake Spirits ne're been higher rear'd
> With stronger blood, we should have answer'd Heaven
> Boldly, not guilty; the Imposition clear'd
> Hereditarie ours.

Hermione draws the obvious conclusion that 'You have trip'd since', and his reply makes it clear that they 'tript' by marriage and that he was equating sexual immaturity with paradisal innocence, which, if preserved, would have freed them from orginal sin (the 'hereditary imposition'). Their wives were the 'Temptations have since been borne to's'. The loss of sexual innocence, even in virtuous and loving marriage, is regarded as a sort of acceptance of the taint of man's 'hereditary' sin. All this is part of a conversation between two people both of whose marriages (up to that point) are deeply satisfactory, and which consists mostly of the sort of mild joking and teasing that goes on between old friends. The assumption that sex – even in a chaste marriage – is essentially corrupt and sinful is so ingrained in the thinking of the time that the idea arouses no particular emotion, either of guilt, or disgust, or even of desire to contradict.

This assumption that loss of virginity is a loss of personal value is allied to the superstitious feeling that virginity is likely to be lost, so that a claim to be virgin is suspect. The medieval moral sense was preoccupied with the notion of the power and persuasiveness of evil, and this evil was envisaged in a Manichean manner as a Power in its own right, opposed to the power of God. This went along with the virtual identification of evil with the body already referred to, so it is not hard to see why sexual integrity was immediately and obsessively suspect. Hamlet's immediate reaction to Ophelia's claim to be 'honest' is that since she is also 'fair' her 'honesty' isn't likely to last long. He also indicates that she unconsciously wants to lose her innocence, since she behaves in a seductive way: 'you jig, you amble and you lispe, and nickname God's creatures, and make your Wantonness, your Ignorance'. Here, also, it is not extra-marital sex that Hamlet is talking about, but just sex. He wants her to go to a nunnery: 'Why wouldst thou be a breeder of sinners?' 'I say, we will have no more marriages.' Certainly, in this scene Hamlet is pretending to be mad, but the assumptions he makes about sex are not evidence of his madness. His madness (if it is madness, which his uncle appears to doubt) consists in so easily saying and acting on emotions that are better kept quiet.

Leontes, in *The Winter's Tale*, suspects his wife of unfaithfulness on no evidence at all, and piles up 'proofs' from outward signs of innocence, as Hamlet does, interpreting them as dissembling their opposites. This mentality is the same that is evident in some of the witchcraft trials of the Middle Ages. Signs or protestations of innocence were taken as proofs of duplicity and therefore of guilt – beauty being especially suspect, as in Ophelia's case.

In a more innocent context, maidenhood is a subject for constant jokes in the plays. One typical example is a light, bawdy interchange between Benedick and Margaret in *Much Ado About Nothing*. The puns and allusions are concerned with foils, swords, buckles and pikes which are, Benedick says, 'dangerous weapons for maids'. For the virgin's vulnerable condition, which in tragic situations arouses reverence or suspicion, is more commonly a subject for jokes. It is suggested by Eric Partridge (in *Shakespeare's Bawdy*) that the plays that display sexual revulsion most clearly belong to a phase in Shakespeare's own life when personal circumstances induced such a feeling. This found ready expression in the anti-sex doctrines of his culture, but that was not his normal outlook. The balance of feeling, in the plays, is on the side of normal, everyday sensual chat. This shows that we should be careful before we interpret the many clerical effusions on sex, or the morbid obsessions of witch-hunters and inquisitors, as sufficient indications of the everyday attitudes of ordinary people. The sexual obsessions of the Middle Ages are not in dispute, but it is always necessary to notice how human beings seem to have a built in counter-balance to doctrines that patently damage human life and intercourse. Most of the time, for most people, the fear of sex and the attempt to restrict and suppress it is only marginally effective. The doctrine may be accepted, but this acceptance itself may draw the sting of the doctrine, as when Hermione teases Polixenes about his 'sin'. She may call it a sin but she doesn't find any difficulty in reconciling such a use of words with a deep and mature appreciation of the joy and satisfaction of sexual love in marriage. Real life examples, such as the warm married love evident in some of the Paston letters, and Eloise's pride and pleasure in the memory of her love for Abelard (even though she repents the element she refers to as 'sin') show the same ability to live with a contradiction between doctrine and experience. Joking is one way of releasing any tension arising from this situation, and Shakespeare's bawdy consists very largely of jokes – aristocratically witty or more broadly humorous – that do just that. But at this Shakespearian point the contradiction is no longer merely implicit, he forces recognition of it. It is by this sign that we may recognize the cultural revolution I referred to earlier. The recognizable range of human emotion was no longer able to accommodate itself within the accepted doctrines. Accumulated experiences, perceived and expressed by poets and thinkers, were too strong to be lived 'on the side' or lumped together under the heading of 'sin'.

It is difficult to quote particular passages to illustrate this recognition of powerful but unofficial influences, because they show themselves more in the general mood than in distinct passages. In a stage of cultural transition this is likely to be so, because the language in current use is the one formed by the preconceptions of the past. New ideas at first make themselves felt mainly 'between the lines', in situations and behaviour rather than words. From many possible examples, a few must be enough to indicate the sort of thing I mean. In the Middle Ages it was always common to make fun of the hypocrisy of the cleric who denounced and persecuted sexual sin but was himself a lecher in private. But of Angelo in *Measure for Measure*, as even the outraged Isabella admits, 'A due sinceritie governed his deedes, Till he did looke on me.' Lucio sketches Angelo in two inimitable passages. The first describes what appears to be the medieval ascetic ideal, to which many naturally warm-blooded men mistakenly aspired in vain, a sexless being, untroubled by normal emotion and desire:

> a man whose blood
> Is very snow-broth; one, who never feeles
> The wanton stings and motions of the sence,
> But doth rebate, and blunt his naturall edge
> With profits of the mind: Studie and fast.

The second (being addressed to a male and not to Isabella who might have been shocked) could not possibly be interpreted as admiring. Considering the icy integrity of the man, this *homme moyen sensuel* remarks that

> They say this Angelo was not made by Man and Woman, after this downeright way of Creation. . . . Some report, a Sea-maid spawn'd him; some, that he was begot betweene two Stock-fishes. But it is certaine that when he makes water his Urine is congeal'd ice; that I know to bee true.

This, or something of similar import if less pithily expressed, might have been said in any medieval tavern where men expressed their opinion of the celibate whom official doctrine obliged them to admire. They would either despise his lack of virility or suppose his chastity to be false. But Angelo's attempt on the virtue of the novice Isabella is not due to any hypocrisy. He is as horrified at the desire he discovers in himself as any of those who learn of it later.

> Ever till now,
> When men were fond [in love], I smild, and wondred how.

He is also surprised (as we smug post-Freudians are not)

that Isabella's religious virginity rouses his desire, where the allurements of a more openly sexy woman would merely have disgusted him.

> Can it be
> That modesty may more betray our Sence,
> Than woman's lightnesse? . . .
> What dost thou, or what art thou, Angelo?
> Dost thou desire her fowly for those things,
> That make her good?

The poor man, who thought himself above temptation, is genuinely appalled. The psychological subtlety of poor Angelo's repressed sexuality shows a new attitude to human emotion. Perhaps sex is corrupting, this play seems to say, but repudiation of sex may not be the best way to deal with the situation.

The Winter's Tale is my final example, perhaps a rather obvious one, but it is interesting because the suspicion/reconciliation plot follows a classic medieval pattern, yet within this frame a new sexual attitude becomes apparent. Leontes' groundless jealousy of the virtuous Hermione tests her love and faithfulness, and she endures for sixteen years. It is the theme of 'Patient Griselda' and of many ballad tales of faithful women brutally tested by suspicious lovers or husbands. Faithfulness and patience win the reward of final reconciliation and reinstatement. But there is a great difference in the psychological pattern of relationships in Shakespeare's play. It seems that Leontes' jealousy is aroused (although he does not realize this) by Hermione's frank and whole-hearted acceptance of the joys of sex in her marriage. Her talk with her husband and his friend is full of sexual overtones which are enthusiastic, rather than shaded with shame or reluctance as the traditional doctrine would dictate. Leontes, not yet really suspicious, and roused by this atmosphere of marital warmth, reminds her of the time when

Three crabbed Moneths had souwr'd themselves to death,
Ere I could make thee open thy white Hand,
And clap thy self my Love; then didst thou utter
I am yours for ever.

There is a beautiful contrast between the shrivelled, dis-
agreeable ('crabbed', from crab-apples, which are sour and
wrinkled) state of the unmarried, and the generous unrestrained
promise of love symbolized by the opened hand – white,
with its reminder of unspotted virginity. But it is this very
mood of open appreciation of sexual love, in himself echoing
Hermione's, that rouses all the medieval devils in Leontes and
drives him to tyranny, treachery, and two attempts at murder.
There is nothing whatever that could make him suspect
Hermione's virtue except her attitude to sex – and that means
sex with himself. But that makes it worse. He is punishing her,
but also himself, for not finding sex shameful. There must be
something wicked about it, says the medieval conscience, and
if I can't see anything I must simply assume it's disguised.

This is a much more subtle presentation of a sexual situation
than the traditional theme of the wronged wife. It is an
attack on the morality that cast a shadow of shame over the
marriage bed. Hermione's apparent death exorcised the devils
of sexual fear, and made Leontes realize his own neurotic
obsession, with astonishment and horror.

Among Shakespeare's ambiguous sexual attitudes we can
recognize the birth of a new sexual doctrine. But if the
Renaissance ferment made it possible for it to be born, the
medieval mood, with all its sexual sickness, must have been
pregnant with it. Hermione's notion of sex is so maturely
integrated into married life as a whole that she would, one
feels, have been as puzzled and shocked to hear it discussed in
isolation, as she was bewildered to find herself accused. Sex
as such did not occupy her mind. Her husband did. Angelo,
on the other hand, was incapable of linking sex and person,

either in his rejection or in his lust, but was obsessed with it, in truly medieval fashion. To him, Claudio the sexual offender is simply a puppet labelled 'fornicator'. Isabella is equally a puppet – a body, which (to his own horror) he happens to want. Yet in the medieval reverence for virginity, which is still so apparent in Shakespeare's England, there is the necessary beginning of Hermione's mature sexuality. If a girl's virginity, or the virtue of a wife, are damaged then the *person* is damaged. Virtue is not simply a commercial commodity for upper-class girls, as in ancient Rome or some Polynesian tribes; it has to do with the person.

This is of crucial importance. I shall be looking, in the next chapter, at the cultivation of sex and it will be interesting to see whether it produces any greater realization of sex as personal than the medieval desire to suppress it. Shakespeare, interpreting the insights of his age with far greater explicitness than most of his contemporaries were able to do, drew on the medieval cult of virginity, implicitly condemning its evils, as in Angelo, but also recognizing (as the medieval writers themselves did not) that this reverence indirectly emphasized the value of the individual person, regardless of their sexual usefulness or the commercial value of their virgin condition. There is no suggestion anywhere in Shakespeare or his contemporaries that loss of virginity outside marriage is merely loss of bridal market value. Shakespeare's developed value for whole human individuals was therefore the true child of the Christian, not the pagan, type of reverence for virginity. For in spite of the obsessions and superstitions which the medieval Church embraced and acted upon with such vigour, the Church as an organization was committed to a doctrine which gave immense value to the individual person, since this person, soul and body, was capable of salvation – that is, of sharing in the life of the Godhead. And this theory was maintained with obstinate consistency through all the failures to recognize its practical implications or do anything about them, and indeed through the pursuance of policies totally opposed to any such idea, for at the same time the Church itself held up to admiration the ascetic excesses of penitents, and surrounded the sex act even in marriage with a host of conditions and regulations based on the notion that it was essentially unclean. It might have been expected, in the anti-sex culture of the time, that the doctrine of the resurrection of the body which involves the conviction that the human body is essentially holy, and is one whole with the animating 'soul', would gradually die out and be replaced by teaching more in accordance with the prejudices and fears of the time. It did not, and the writings of truly good and loving Christians of this period – celibate or not – attest the continuance of this theological assertion of the value of the whole person, body and soul. Contemporary letters show warm friendships between people of opposite sex, in which no sign of sex worries is apparent. The letters of Blessed Jordan of Saxony (successor of St Dominic) to Diana D'Andolo, whose career as head of a new convent he supported, are full of frank affection, tender teasing and the confidence of friends. They are 'love' letters in a wider and more human sense than many of those usually so called, although these two were celibate. In such people the continuing doctrine of human value is apparent. So at the end of all this there emerged, stronger and more durable than the arrogant sexual licence of Renaissance cynicism, the slow-growing doctrine of maturity and wholeness in love which is first apparent in Shakespeare. It remained, however, an ideal which was appreciated explicitly by few. If Shakespeare can be said to show the birth of the notion of mature love, with which the medieval world had been uncomfortably pregnant, I may perhaps extend the metaphor and wonder why the infant was for so long sickly and neglected, so that significant growth and development belong to a time four centuries later.

The break-up of medieval Europe cannot be assigned to any one cause. The Black Death, the rise of the merchant classes and the urban artisan class, the corruption of the Church, and therefore the emergence of more effective leaders among secular princes – all these disrupted the system from within. The network of social responsibility, badly neglected but still in existence, broke down with it. The final destruction of this sense of 'belonging' which had in any case been so corrupted and abused as to have become more harmful than helpful, left a spiritual vacuum, and it had to be filled. It was filled by a new attitude which made each one responsible not only for his own relation to God in faith, as in the new Reformed tradition, but also economically responsible for himself and his family. It was the only possible attitude in such a situation, for to lack independence was to go under. None need expect support if he could not support himself, and vagrancy and begging became crimes. People might give 'charity' to the poor, but it was an extra. The medieval sense that the rich man ought to give all 'surplus' (i.e. non-essential wealth) to the poor (constantly preached as an unquestioned moral law though as often ignored) had disappeared entirely. In such an atmosphere the sense of family assumed importance, and the alliance of capitalism with the morality of the 'closed' patriarchal family became inevitable, for the sake of survival. This may help to account for the shift in sexual restriction from an emphasis on virginity to an emphasis on domestic virtue. The medieval family was not an economic unit and the mutual support of blood-relations was not necessary for survival. It is interesting that, although the medieval wife's sexual lapses were sinful and punishable (she was, after all, her husband's property), they did not have a 'taboo' character, since open force could be used, if necessary, to keep her in her place. The Puritan wife, however, was both more essential to the emotional security of the family and less subject to coercion, because coercion could not preserve the emotional bond that was so vital in a world where only the family could give security. Her virtue, therefore, was protected by repulsions of a 'taboo' type, much stronger than those surrounding her medieval sister.

But both types of society had an interest in sexual repulsion, though for rather different reasons, and the capitalist–Puritan version appears to have been rather a detour than the main road. I would suggest, tentatively, that the notion of personal value in medieval spirituality was actually enabled to discover its own true meaning in terms of a mature notion of human love, by the impact of the Renaissance rediscovery of Greek exaltation of man. But the possible further development of this understanding, foreshadowed by John Donne, of the beauty of married sex, was prevented, or at least postponed, by the pressure of the economic changes I have mentioned. It continued to develop, but very slowly, and only among an élite. These were people who did not have to engage in the ruthless struggle for the financial security that could give one the right to be regarded as a full member of society, since they already had it. For the 'lower classes', in this age, were not regarded as fully human. Only property gave one that status and it was only when the struggle of what Raymond Williams called 'The Long Revolution' had transformed the social structure of English life that ordinary people became able to consider sexuality and marriage in terms of a fully human relationship. This process has not gone very far yet, and the upheaval it is causing is obvious. The attempt to recast divorce laws in relation to the value of the relationships and not primarily in relation to notions of sexual sin is one sign of the upheaval in sexual attitudes, and the controversies over it show the unfinished nature of the changes that are taking place.

SEXUAL LOVE:
THE CULTIVATION OF SEX

AFTER a look at what happens to love when sex is repressed, a little study of times and places in which sex is welcomed and even cultivated with enthusiasm may seem to offer a pleasant change. There is certainly a complete change of atmosphere, but whether it favours the growth of love is another matter.

The societies and groups that approve of sex show an even wider range of motives and attitudes than do those that repress it. There are many variations, but in order to avoid being either too unwieldy or too anecdotal, it is helpful to divide them into four main types of approval of sex.

The first of these might be called the pragmatic attitude. It finds sex pleasant as well as useful for procreation. Sex is treated as the most naturally enjoyable (and inexpensive) of pastimes and therefore restrictions are imposed on it only in certain well-defined circumstances, of which there are generally few. It therefore cultivates the technique of sex to a greater or lesser extent. The second regards sex as sacred, a means of linking human beings with the divine, and sometimes as the way in which the divinity exercises its power over creation, both human, animal and vegetable. The sexual act in this view is, or on occasions can be, a cultic act, an act of worship. The third attitude is the exploitative, and it is mainly a male one, though certain women can do very well out of it financially. It regards sex as an escape from boredom, frustration, as a sign of the rejection of restrictive codes and values, an assertion of autonomy and personal power and value. The fourth attitude is the 'romantic' and it might be described as the cultivation of sexual desire, rather than of sex, since the focus of interest is the emotion of passionate desire, which is cultivated in a spirit that can only be described as religious. The consummation of the union is not stressed, and may be deliberately postponed or even forbidden.

These four categories are not exclusive, except occasionally in small societies free from, or indifferent to, outside influence. It is more usual for the main tendency to be modified by different influences from those that produced its central 'doctrines'. In a large and complex society made up of many cultural influences, social layers and types of economic inter-relations, it may be difficult to identify the leading doctrine with any certainty. The effect of this multiplication of influences is not only to make it hard, even for the members of the society concerned, to recognize and articulate their own type of sexual doctrine, it also means that the safeguards that may be built into a unitary society to counteract undesirable effects of its permitted range of sexual behaviour are absent. There is, in fact, no clear and accepted code of sexual be-haviour, but only a vague and often inarticulate conglomera-tion of assumptions and feelings. This applies to the restrictive as well as to the approving attitudes to sex, and this over-lapping of types of attitude can also mean the overlapping of approving and disapproving types in the same society and even in the same person. For instance, the puritan and the romantic are often combined, likewise the ascetic and the exploitative, as in Shakespeare's Angelo. But just because human attitudes to sex are in practice seldom formed by unitary cultural conditioning, it is helpful to separate the various strands in order to understand better how they combine in, for instance, the contemporary European scene, and how much love goes into the sexual yarn which is so important a part of the fabric of our, or any other, society.

An example of the first kind of sexual 'doctrine' is that of some Polynesian tribes. There used to be more difference between the cultures and mores of the various islands than many people realize, but by and large we should be correct in describing them all as 'permissive' societies. Many anthropologists have been fascinated by the Samoans in particular, and the literature devoted to them is huge and growing. The availability of scholarly observations has not, however, succeeded in destroying the myth of the guilt-free, 'natural' islanders, living in a state of paradisal innocence, untainted by the anxieties and obsessions laid on Western man by Christianity, civilization, capitalism – take your choice; whatever the favourite villain, the Samoans could be held up as an example of how blissful human life would be if only he were destroyed. It is probable that the need for such a myth would have ensured its acceptance and preservation in any case. The 'noble savage' has to be invented if he doesn't exist, in every brooding, over-organized society. But the spell that the islands threw over several European visitors who wrote about them, and the fact that by the time more objective observers appeared alien government had stamped out certain traditional features of island life, may have helped to present a picture of virtually unshadowed happiness. But whatever may be the final verdict, there is no doubt that the age-old myth of a 'golden age' found a very plausible symbol in the Samoan people.

For a start they were, and are, beautiful. They were unshy, hospitable, gentle, and obviously enjoyed life. And on closer investigation there seemed every reason why they should. The climate was pleasant, and food so easy to obtain that very little labour was required in order to satisfy everyone. The organization of labour and of possessions was therefore minimal, and there was no incentive to seek for a political power which would be meaningless. In such a situation, the tendency to regard wives as essential economic props, whose loss or unreliability threatened the existence of the family, was naturally absent. Women worked, but the loose groupings of large extended families in the villages, meant that no particular woman was indispensable either economically or, consequently, emotionally. The wife was not a possession to be jealously guarded, because no one else was particularly likely to covet her. If a wife had a few affairs with men other than her husband no one worried, and the husband frequently had a few of his wife's sisters as extra wives, with her full approval. He would offer his wife for a visitor's use as part of his hospitality, and *she* was offended if the offer were refused. Children were cared for by a large number of women and little girls besides the mother, and family relationships (though the patterns vary and are very complex) were never intense. In such a society, casual sex does not threaten the social order. The upper-class girl was required to be a virgin, but this was the sole example of the way economic pressures regulate sexual behaviour in a negative sense, since the girl's virginity was a feature of the social prestige she brought to her husband, for which he was prepared to pay a considerable amount. The pre-marital virginity of the daughters of the village high chiefs also served as a symbol of the 'intactness' of other marriageable girls, who were not required to be virgins, but still held that status in some sense. This genial and well-understood fiction was all part of the accommodation to life of a society in which strong emotions and ambitions would be not only useless – since there was enough for all with minimum effort – but even dangerous. If passions and energies cannot serve a useful purpose they are bound to be destructive, therefore in this society everything was organized so as to minimize personal emotion and easy sex was vital to the viability of the social organism. Once more, economic considerations dictate sexual behaviour but this time in the direction of permissiveness, not repression. Margaret Mead describes it thus:

In Samoa, the expected personality is one to which sex will be a delightful experience, expertly engaged in, one which still will not be sufficiently engrossing to threaten the social order. The Samoans condone light love-affairs, but repudiate acts of passionate choice, and have no real place for anyone who would permanently continue, in spite of social experience to the contrary, to prefer one woman or one man to a more socially acceptable mate. The demand that one should be both receptive to the advances of many lovers and yet capable of showing the tokens of virginity at marriage is sufficiently incompatible, and was solved first by placing the onus of virginity not on the whole young female population, but on the *taupou*, the ceremonial princess of the village. She was then better guarded than the other girls and so freed from temptation. As an additional precaution, the blood of virginity could always be counterfeited. The *taupou* who failed to warn her chaperones that she was not a *taupou* and so on her wedding-night shamed the village, risked being beaten to death – not for her frailty but for her failure to make an adequate provision of chicken blood.

(This was not as difficult to arrange as the 'virginity' of girls put up for sale as virgins in eighteenth-century brothels, since there was no question of the hymen being broken by intercourse. It was a chief, or official 'counsellor' who broke it, in public, with two fingers bound in white bark-cloth, which he then held up to the assembled company so that they could see the blood. In some places the girl was paraded, naked and still bleeding, before her new relatives. It should be added that it appears that some tribes were less accommodating than the one Margaret Mead studied, and the girl really had to be virgin, or suffer death.)

Marriages were arranged between families, with some attention to the wishes of the young, and the young in turn conducted with suitable partners the long liaisons that led to pregnancy and were regarded as appropriate preparations for marriage, and reserved quick affairs 'under the palm-trees' for the unsuitable mates. Pre-marital affairs and extra-marital affairs were conducted with enough lightness not to threaten the reliable sex relationships between married couples, sex relationships so reliable that they have now underwritten one of the highest population increases recorded in the modern world.

But this natural result of a great deal of easy and pleasurable sex points to a fact about the quality of life in such a culture which is extremely relevant to this study. The continued existence of this way of life depended on the fact that there was enough for everyone. An enormous increase in number of children would inevitably threaten the standard of living in an economy with limited land, and neither desire for, nor possibility of, significant change or expansion of the economy by way of trade. The answer to this was simple. Certain hit-or-miss methods of abortion were common, but the easiest method of controlling population increase was by killing unwanted babies. Before infanticide was suppressed by the foreign governments (New Zealand and the United States) who administered the islands under League of Nations Mandate this was quite normal, usually done by strangling. Commonly, the mother did it herself; one woman, when questioned, said she had killed seventeen of her babies. She may have been exaggerating, but there is no particular reason why she should. The act carried neither blame nor reward. It was not a crime, or a furtive and desperate expedient, it was not a religious rite or any kind of heroic sacrifice to the common good, it was not even a traditional tribal custom, as in the New Guinea tribe that demanded that each woman kill her first baby and suckle a young pig in its place. It was simply an unfortunate social necessity.

Perhaps this long-standing custom, which proved difficult

to eradicate because the Samoans could not understand why the foreigners disapproved of it, goes some way to answering the question implicit in the inclusion of the Samoans in this brief study. Do people love each other in this kind of society? If we can accept my tentative definition of love, as a reaching out towards something further and deeper in human life, then the answer must be that there was very little of it in Samoa. The whole of life was organized in such a way as to dissipate and blunt any such drive, for the sake of the stability of the common life. There was certainly a great deal of solid human affection, but this was prevented from becoming deep and demanding by the spreading of emotional ties over a large number of people, and the provision of easy and immediate reduction of marital tensions by the introduction of an extra partner or two. The deepening and intensification of a human relationship, or the intensification of any human desire, comes about when it overcomes obstacles, thus breaking down psychological barriers of inertia or timidity or selfishness, and releasing greater spiritual power. This is recognized by virtually all religions and cultural systems that encourage the 'reaching out' of the spirit, and it is a fact taken into account, unconsciously, by systems that canalize it (as in religion or the arts) or exploit it (as in work or war). In Samoa this was never allowed to 'build up' to a degree where it could achieve anything, either in personal relationships, or in the arts, or in (say) some kind of mysticism. Even warfare was reduced to a more or less formal affair, and gossip or manoeuvre for local political advantage was the most effective form that aggression was likely to take. All emotions, in fact, were deflected and diluted. Contrary to the western myth, the Samoans were as unromantic as any people could be. Their pleasure in sex was as simple, open and superficial as a child's pleasure in licking an ice-cream cone.

This does not mean that no love existed. The very care that

was taken to discourage it shows that it was recognized (unconsciously) as a real danger. In the respectable nineteenth-century culture there were many ways in which people did manage to love each other, either with real (though inarticulate) sexual love or with a love that managed to 'get round' the distaste for sex and flourish in spite of it. The human need to love is infinitely adaptable. In the same way, even in a society that discouraged it as thoroughly as the Samoan one did, people managed to love. But the Samoan idyll turns out, on examination, to be not so much a state of paradisal innocence and pleasure as a well organized, down to earth system for living as well as possible in certain well-defined conditions. It was quite ruthless, when necessary, in exacting the type of behaviour that made this possible. There was no room for the non-conformist in this paradise.

This Samoan culture (which is now so modified by other influences that it has virtually disappeared) is useful to our understanding of sexual attitudes because of its unitary character. It shows the 'pragmatic' approach to sex in as pure a form as possible, and in doing so shows the unconscious ulterior motive which actually belies the description of it as 'pragmatic'. It shows the falseness of the romantic European notion that only the *repression* of sex is artificial or motivated by considerations other than those of the value of the experience.

The 'pragmatic' approach is not confined to isolated 'primitive' cultures. As E. P. Thompson makes clear in his *The Making of the English Working Class* a very similar attitude prevailed in English villages and small towns among working-class people before the Industrial Revolution. In a life consisting of hard but not interminable work, with a sparse but reasonable standard of living, sex was a recognized pastime and most girls were pregnant before marriage – indeed this proof of fertility was required by a man who wanted a wife who would bear him the children needed to make the family economically viable in an agricultural, or home-industry, economy. But this was not a 'unitary' society and the relaxed and earthy attitude to sex was combined, in many odd ways, with at least nominal Christianity, so that pre-marital sex was carried on in secluded places, and not publicly acknowledged, though it might be gossiped about freely. Extramarital sex was, however, not normally acceptable. The ban on adultery (particularly of the wife) was enforced by the usual mixture of religious repulsion and economic need for family stability, each reinforcing the other. So sexual emotions were not always light, and sexual jealousy was a frequent theme of songs, together with stories of passion and murder, rape, infanticide (from despair of discovery not as a form of birth-control) and suicide. The Samoans would never have understood such emotions.

Another kind of influence was also at work, which helped to prevent such violent sexual emotions from getting out of hand by giving them recognized (by the villagers, that is, if not by the 'gentry') outlets in seasons of festival when a certain amount of sexual licence was part of the general jollification. It was for this reason that moralists, both religious and secular, tried to stamp out such customs as 'wakes' and the various festive seasons of Christmas, Shrove-tide and so on at which there was usually a fair. These fairs were the especial target of those who wished to suppress the Vices of the Poor. They were occasions for serious trade, but also they were breaks in the routine of hard work and poor living, times of better food (saved up for with much care), of meeting and dancing and the buying of frivolities like ribbons for the girls and toys and sweets for the children. But they were also occasions of sexual horseplay and fun, and Thompson quotes a description of Whit Monday from a Northumberland diarist in 1750: 'Abundance of young men and women diverted themselves with the game or pastime here that they call Losing their Suppers. . . . And after all they ended their recreation with carrouzing at the Ale-houses and ye men Kissing and toying away most of the night with their mistresses.' He also quotes a Bolton magistrate's disapproving description of 'a very large procession of young men and women with fiddles, garlands, and other ostentation of rural finery, dancing Morris dances in the highway merely to celebrate an idle anniversary.' This, and many other descriptions of country customs at festival times, show that they are direct descendants of pagan customs and feasts, associated with fertility rites for various times of year. The magistrate quoted was especially annoyed because this levity occurred at a time when there was serious hardship in the area, and it made no sense to him that the country people should disport themselves in their 'finery' when they should have been working all the harder in order to grow more or earn more. But the crises of sexual licence at certain times, in the context of religious celebrations, are in fact characteristic of societies whose living is hard and uncertain. So the eighteenth-century English rural economy shows the mingling of at least three different types of sexual attitude – the repressive (from its medieval Christian background of sexual repulsion as well as from the less exotic Protestant teaching against sex outside marriage), the pragmatic (to the degree to which life was reasonably secure and relaxed) and also the one that I propose to study next, which regards sex as in some sense sacred. The recognized sexual horseplay of the seasonal celebrations in England was not, of course, consciously connected with any such idea, but the roots of it are clear.

One example of a society in which sex had a sacred function was the Babylonian. Like all cultures in which the economy is basically agricultural, the religious observances were connected with the cycle of the seasons, and their purpose was to ensure the fertility of the land, the cattle, and also the people. No fears of over-population haunted a people inhabiting a wide country whose prosperity at home, and defences from (or conquest of) enemies abroad depended on a rising birth-rate. Among the important yearly festivals was one at which a man and woman enacted the union of the god and goddess An and his consort Innana. The idea is similar to that of 'sympathetic' magic. The human act not only presents ritually but also in some sense *brings about* the event at the divine level, and this was vital because the fertility of the land depended on the union of the gods. This festival was an occasion for a great deal of drinking and licensed sexual freedom, in a country where at other times sex was under the control of reasonably strict marriage laws.

Innana, the goddess of fertility, became Ishtar of the Akkadians (Astarte in Greek). Her worship spread with the imperial expansion of Assyria and Babylonia, and as it spread many local fertility cults faded into it, or it into them. In particular she took over from the great mother goddess Asherah, also goddess of the sea, who was worshipped in Tyre and Sidon. Her shrines were scattered throughout Phoenicia and Syria, little country sanctuaries in the open air and often on top of a hill, and marked by some kind of pillar of stone or wood. No one knows exactly what these were, for none survive, but they were known as 'Asheram', and were centres of local seasonal feasts, burial cults and so on. These 'high places' were repeatedly denounced by the Hebrew prophets whose people lived alongside the Canaanites. The Hebrews lived the same life as their 'pagan' neighbours, and found their cult linked to the seasonal cycle, and expressed in easily grasped myths and rituals, much more to their taste than the austere theology of the imageless, nameless, sexless God of Moses and the prophets, who demanded moral rectitude and was apparently unbribeable. The prophets make it clear that they objected especially to the sexual goings-on at the 'high places', which were probably a countrified version of the usual fertility rituals with their recognized and temporary sexual licence. This disapproval of the prophets has been held to be just another example of the Judaeo-Christian puritanical disapproval of sex. But in fact the Jewish law about sex and marriage only tightened up at a much later period, and the 'puritanical' attitude can be seen developing in the 'Wisdom' literature after the Exile. At this earlier time, although adultery was punishable, Hebrew men had several wives and concubines if they liked, and prostitutes were normal. But these were 'ordinary' prostitutes, there to satisfy ordinary lust. What the prophets objected to about the fertility rites was not sexual licence as such but the fact that it was a form of worship of the idol, the 'Asherah'. It was thus a union with the foreign god, and an act of apostasy to Yahweh. To see the Canaanites as a jolly, permissive people, and the Hebrews as (if their religious leaders got their way) a strait-laced, guilt-ridden collection of pilgrim-fathers is to read the situation in terms of our own prejudices. Actually, normal Canaanite marriage laws, and sanctions, were similar to those of their Hebrew neighbours.

These rural celebrations lacked the clear theological definition which explained the organized temple prostitution of the great coastal shrines of Ishtar-Astarte (who had taken over from Asherah). Sacred prostitution is especially associated with Astarte, and later on Aphrodite took it over. By the time the huge temple of Aphrodite at Acro-Corinth became famous for its thousands of girls dedicated to the goddess, it seems possible that the religious ideal had been debased into little more than a superstition, but the great shrines of Astarte had been places of solemn and vitally important service to the goddess on whom life depended. Prostitutes could be of either sex. In Babylon unmarried girls were expected to serve

F

in the temple in this capacity, waiting for a male worshipper to choose them, for ritual intercourse, after which they returned home. In India this custom was still preserved at least until recently, but it was the permanent priests of the temple who performed the act with women who came to worship.

One could go on quoting examples endlessly, since so many cultures in so many places have included ritual intercourse as an important part of their religion, as a means to ensure fertility for the land and the people, or as a personal act of devotion, from a desire for communion with the god. Both these ideas generally enter in, but roughly speaking the former predominates in earlier cultures with a clearer sense of corporate being, while the second is more explicit in Greece and Rome, when a deep and anxious curiosity about the private identity and existence of man had begun to make itself felt.

The organized and solemn temple rituals are a different thing from the occasional festivals of the countryside, though the temples were also centres for seasonal celebrations. The need for a periodic outlet of emotions – of lust or of hate, or both – which are necessarily suppressed at other times seems to belong to popular cultures. These are either in a subsistence economy in the country areas, where heavy and unending work leaves scant regular leisure, and the hazards of nature undermine the sense of security, or among urban poor who again have little leisure, no security, and no supportative religious belief to make constant fear, want and oppression bearable. In Imperial Rome these 'outlets' for the poor were more or less secular and became more and more debased, but in the country and in earlier times they were associated firmly with worship, and therefore even their most violent forms were fitted into the scheme of life of men and gods, and were followed by a sense of peace and reconciliation with nature and with oneself. The Dionysiac outbreaks were probably of this kind, and the frenzy of the god's votaries, however disgusting it may appear to us, was in fact a healing and peace-bringing act. They were probably originally part of the country fertility cults, but as time went on they became dissociated from seasonal celebrations and agricultural centres. They acquired more of the character of the search for divine union and were confined to groups of initiates, mostly women. Later on they became less exclusive, and were 'patronized' by well-to-do people. But by this time they were no longer a popular cult and, like the recent interest in witchcraft and exotic cults among well-to-do Europeans, served as a release no longer from the fears and burdens of poverty, but from the anxieties uncovered in the comparatively affluent by the very removal of everyday economic pressures.

Whatever the economic reasons for the type of cultic sex that occurs, or the varieties of practice and of the myths that underwrite the practice, the common element is some view of sex as a link with the divine. This view can be described as sacramental, but it would be a mistake to assume that in societies where the religious practice includes sexual rituals the view of 'everyday' sex is necessarily coloured by this. In some cultures there is a considerable homogeneity in religious and secular life, but this often means not so much that daily life has a religious character as that the whole culture has a magical style. In Babylonia, for instance, a high level of cultural achievement was combined with an anthropomorphic type of religion in which every stone had its own life, and every human action was weighted with the good or ill will of many spirits. Amulets, charms and endless magical rites preserved health and sanity, and sex was particularly fertile ground for magical beliefs. There is no evidence, however, that normal intercourse between husband and wife, for instance, had any sacramental significance. This seems to have been true of most cultures, both primitive and highly evolved, in which the sexual rites of religion held a really important place in the life of the natives or tribe. This is perhaps because the very corporate feeling which makes it possible to accept that the ritual acts of a few people, or on a few occasions, can vitally affect the whole people, also makes it impossible to suppose that the individual as such can 'get through' to his gods. Contact with the divine is purely through ritual, in which one may take part at certain times, or perhaps only observe. In his private life the individual as such does not worship.

In the culture of classical Greece, however, a different idea seems to emerge. Earlier Greek religion appears to have been of a rural fertility type similar to those of other agricultural economies, with certain cult centres at which annual festivals were more elaborately celebrated. As the culture of the cities developed, in which the economy was less subject to seasonal fluctuations and less threatened by natural disaster, this type of religion was allowed to retire to the country. For the Athenians, religious ritual was an expression of passionate civic loyalty and pride embodied in the gods with their magnificent temples and rites. At the same time there was increasing speculation about the nature of man, life, death and the gods. The lessened anxiety about survival due to an assured political position and flourishing economy meant that an intense corporate consciousness was not necessary. In this more relaxed climate personal experience became something to be observed and discussed. It is in such a climate of thought that the notion emerges of the direct influence of the divine on the individual, even of the divine presence in a person. It is still thought of as 'possession' or protection or election by some god or goddess, but this is not confined to people with special cultic and representational functions, like priests and priestesses, or people enacting divine roles in the rites. The Greeks detected the action and presence of the gods in human activities that were not explicable in terms of reasonably motivated behaviour, and also in states of mind that could not be attained by conscious decision but apparently 'descended' on people or 'seized' them. Madness or frenzy were regarded as evidence of divine influence (and were not, therefore, shameful) but drunkenness was also a way to come *hors de soi* and therefore be in contact with the divine. The passion of love – what we call 'being in love' – came under the heading of madness, but was also, therefore, a sign of possession by the god. And, like drink, sexual intercourse could produce an experience of ecstasy. But the Greeks also recognized the presence of the divine in all that was beautiful, hence the displays of physical grace and prowess which were an important aspect of the great festivals. This feeling, and its link with the gods, was not confined to cultic occasions but coloured the everyday attitude to physical beauty, producing that frank and delicate appreciation of the human body which flowered in the unique artistic achievement of the time. Art, physical display, and the cult of beauty in general were connected with the consciousness of the divine, but in a way that was neither magical (to propitiate powerful spirits) nor precisely religious, if by religious is meant ideas and behaviour with a definite cultic orientation and significance. The Greek love of beauty was not confined to worship but affected civic and domestic art and decoration. In this setting it is not surprising that sex was duly appreciated as a pleasure to be cultivated. But ordinary everyday sex does not seem to have been coloured by the appreciation of sexual 'love' as divine possession, or by the notion that sexual ecstasy was an experience of divine union. This latter idea seems to have been exploited only in a cultic context. Ordinary sex, in fact, was regarded as necessary and pleasurable but undignified and even shameful. This reaction became more intense as time went on. Sexuality, anyway, was strictly for men, and was

categorized in a manner similar to that of nineteenth-century
Europe and America – 'Wives for child-bearing, *hetaerae*
(professional courtesans, often women of considerable culture
and intelligence) for pleasure, and concubines for daily needs.'
If Demosthenes' classification is slightly adapted and we
substitute 'mistresses' for *hetaerae* and 'prostitutes or chamber-
maids' for 'concubines' the parallel is clear. The reason is the
same too. The classical Greek society required warriors, or
warrior-type men, to rule and defend the cities. Departmental-
izing of sexuality seems to be the usual method of preventing
male energy from being concentrated on personal relationships at the expense of civic devotion. The degradation of wives
is part of this programme, and in Greece they were shut up
like lunatics or criminals. One contemporary poem describes
a bride in ecstatic terms, but the poem is by a man who could
not marry her! *Hetaerae* had freedom, but depended on the
favour of their lovers, so that they were often very money-
conscious, and cold to the poor would-be lover. Slaves had
no rights, so that they were always available, but their sub-
human status ruled out any personal relationship. Love for
one's wife was permissible and did exist, and although sex
was not expected to mean much in marriage, there was often
real love and companionship between husband and wife,
as we can see from memorial inscriptions and some touching
poems on dead wives, as well as in good advice to brides.
But the system hardly encouraged such devotion, and the
only kind of close personal relationship that was socially
acceptable was that between men, and especially between an
adult man and a boy. These relationships were lasting and
important. Ideally, they did not include intercourse, indeed
this was forbidden by law, though embraces and 'petting'
were acceptable. *Passion* for a boy was regarded as a 'mania',
like heterosexual passion, and was shameful for a civilized
man. The ideal was perhaps seldom attained, and Cicero's

description of it is probably rose-coloured, but the fact remains that these close and loving relationships were often of great value and are probably responsible for some of the quality of Greek sensibility – its delicacy, ardour, and aesthetic achievement. For here was a *whole* relationship. Such a friendship could be, and was, regarded as under the protection of the gods, and this is as near as the Greeks got to recognizing a sacramental quality in everyday sex. But no intercourse was involved. If it were the relationship was degraded, as it was in heterosexual unions, even though these were regarded as inevitable, and provision made for them. It cannot be said, therefore, that the Greeks had any appreciation of non-cultic sexual acts, with either sex, as sacramental. Rather the contrary.

There was only one voice in the ancient world that stated uncompromisingly that ordinary married sex was sacramental, and it was the voice of one usually denounced as a woman-hater, a puritan and the enemy of all that is natural and pleasant. Paul of Tarsus called married sexual love 'a great sacrament' – the word can also be translated 'mystery', and both mean the same in the Greek, though our usage has separated them. He said that this happened 'in Christ and in the Church' and later, anti-sex Christians made much play with this to show that he 'really' meant that only the union of Christ and the church was the sacrament, and that when, in the same passage, Paul compared human married love and Christ's love he was not referring to anything so sordid as sex but to the 'spiritual' love of man and wife. I have already traced the narrowing of the word 'spirit' in our usage, but in any case Paul made his meaning quite clear, for he used the phrase 'the two shall become one body' (or just 'one', which meant the same thing, since a 'body' was a *person*, not a lump of flesh animated by a 'soul')to describe the union which was 'a great sacrament'. But he used this same phrase to describe intercourse with a prostitute, when he was explaining that it was wrong, not because sex was wrong but because the whole *person* is united with another in intercourse, and the Christian person was united to Christ and should not then be united with a prostitute, with whom, by definition, no love-relationship was created. Christians should marry 'in the Lord', and *this* sexual love was a 'great sacrament'.

However, Paul's doctrine disappeared, submerged by the tide of sexual obsessions that swept Europe. The Fathers had to indulge in incredible mental contortions in order to get Paul on their side against sex, but they managed it, and the anti-sex nature of orthodox Christianity has been one of the main tenets of any respectable anti-Christian creed for centuries – with reason, as the last chapter showed. In the end the sacramental nature of sex, hinted at in Shakespeare and Donne, was reasserted by a man who rejected any recognizable religion, D. H. Lawrence. For Lawrence, sex is *the* sacrament, the significant heart of human experience and the point of growth and maturation. Because of this he dismissed with contempt those who were sexual failures. Lawrence's appreciation of sexuality, like the Greek one, was masculine. The woman's role was essentially to complement the male, and the woman who asserted a personal role or identity other than a purely passive sexual or (temporarily) maternal one was evil and dangerous. But, unlike the Greeks, Lawrence saw sexual intercourse itself as sacramental, and rejected passion without consummation as a perversion. Love, in the sense of an aspiration to further reaches of human experience, made sense to the Greeks, though sexual love in the modern sense did not. To Lawrence, sex made sense but sexual love was suspect, being mixed in his mind with maternal possessiveness, and the fear of being swamped by the woman if she were allowed any personal reality apart from the man. In such a situation, love can be named, and desired, and can even exist precariously, but it cannot grow roots and mature.

Sexual love, then, has done little better in societies that view sex as sacramental than in those that use it with ease and practicality. Paul's teaching never took hold sufficiently to influence the actual nature of the Christian community as such, since the groups were small, and lived by the same daily customs as other people. By the time they had grown large enough to be studied as viable societies the Pauline teaching had succumbed to other doctrines, so there never has been a society in which normal 'domestic' sex has been seriously regarded as sacramental by ordinary people, and we can have no idea what such a society might be like.

In considering sex as sacramental one cannot overlook the cult of sex as a means of communion with evil, rather than with the divine, but there is no place here to do more than mention the continuous existence through the centuries of small groups who used sex as a means of gaining power, opposing 'god', or asserting freedom from normal moral restraint. Witchcraft is the usual name for it. Its most recent, non-religious exponent has been Jean Genet, whose *Thief's Journal* is as revealing as it is revolting in its attempt at total reversal of values. But these doctrines have never carried weight beyond their tiny circles of initiates.

In Greece, the sense of the sacredness of beauty and the divine nature of sexual ecstasy in the cult, faded before the increase of wealth, the decline in prestige and the growing cynicism of the Philosophers – stern moralists though some of them were. Even in the classical period the exploitative attitude to sex had been evident in the use of *hetaerae* and slave girls, but decadent Greece, and later Imperial Rome, became bywords for sexual licence and abuse. There were those who still recognized a divine quality in sexuality, and the cult of Isis was popular in Rome, but the more general attitude to sex was one of a reckless search for means to satiate a lust that (in the absence of other amusements) was increasingly difficult to satisfy. This state of affairs leads to what I called the 'exploitative' attitude to sex. This attitude does not always show such violence and hectic anger, however. The exploitative attitude to sex may simply involve the practice, usual in many types of societies, of regarding certain categories of women as available (whether professionally or not) for the satisfaction of male sexual impulses outside marriage, usually in a quite impersonal way. A good deal of fun can enter into this kind of arrangement, and it may include some friendly and even valuable personal relationship, but more or less accidentally. There may also be an element of aggression in the attitudes of some of those who engage in this kind of sex, and it can include a wide range of perversions and 'specialities'. All the same, the attitude to the women involved, while obviously not respectful or loving (though love may occur exceptionally) is reasonably friendly, appreciative and kind. A man who uses a prostitute doesn't normally want her in his home, but he doesn't hate her. There are many exceptions, but societies that accept prostitution, professional or not, are often (like our own) exploitative only in this sense, that the women – or boys and men – involved are made use of, as a means of pleasure, or the release of tension, or an assertion of that virility which women of 'gentle' breeding tend to bring into doubt. It does not imply a motive of hatred, revenge, or any widespread sadism *as part of the general sexual 'atmosphere'*. A related and quite mild type of the exploitation of sex is well represented by the 'Bunny girl' approach, in which sexual titillation is sufficiently discreet to quiet unruly puritan consciences, while giving a thrill. The 'philosophy' behind the Bunny girls, incidentally, is closer to the 'pragmatic' Samoan view, but the amount of propaganda required to put it over, and the bravado with which it is professed, are sufficient to show that, whatever is said, the sexual feelings of society at large do not easily conform to this pattern. The promoters of the philosophy would like it if they did – or so they say – but the emotional tide does not run that way. This is fortunate for the Bunny clubs, since they would go out of business if sex in the West were accepted in the earthy and unromantic Samoan manner.

The exploitative attitude in its extreme form is a very different matter, and it is not an attitude common to a whole society, but only to certain social groupings within it. The behaviour it dictates makes clear why this is so. A society in which this was the general attitude to sex would collapse in chaos very soon. On the other hand such an attitude on the part of the aristocracy – and it is mainly a phenomenon of the upper classes or of some other élite – naturally affects the attitude of other people who witness it or are aware of it. It is 'in the air' and everyone breathes it.

The example that I have chosen is that of the English upper classes of the eighteenth century. It resembles closely the viciously callous sexual behaviour of the aristocracy of Italy and France at the Renaissance, but eighteenth-century London is better documented than either decadent Rome or Renaissance Tuscany; also it is near to us in time, and cannot be glamourized by its antiquity.

The English-speaking world has recently become re-acquainted with the sexual mores of eighteenth century London, when readers sick of what might be called the 'euphemistic culture' of the early twentieth century welcomed books like *Fanny Hill* for their frank sensuality and humour, and their refusal to be coy. The sheer misery and degradation involved for the women and girls in the 'trade' is easily overlooked. Writers who described London's sexual pastimes if not with whole-hearted approval, at least with amusement and complaisance, were naturally not people likely to care too much about the other side of the picture. This included the kidnapping and sale of little girls to satisfy the lust of men who had tired of older girls. Prepubertal girls fetched a good price, so long as they were virgins, and it was the taking of their maidenhead that provided the really desirable thrill. It was also held to be a cure for venereal disease. Loss of virginity could, however, be made good artificially by means of an operation (no anaesthetics, of course). Nothing so painless as Samoan brides' display of chicken's blood would satisfy the men who demanded unspoiled merchandise, so the brothel-keepers who profited by the transaction obliged the girls to endure this operation over and over again. The girls who were to provide for 'special' needs did not, perhaps, enjoy being whipped, chained, or pricked, though they may have been pleased to retaliate by using the whip on those whose impotence could only be overcome by this means.

The customers for this trade were usually men of the upper classes, rich, but with a wealth that laid on them no requirements of work or responsibility such as the feudal system had laid on even the most brutal and dissolute of landowners. They had no purpose in life, nor, alternatively, any strong religious mystique to give them a *raison d'être* and the stuffing for their self-respect. They belonged within a framework of privilege, whose function had been destroyed by political change, leaving them with no obligations and no hope. They were deeply afraid of this emptiness, and the rigid structure of their upbringing did not usually give them a way out in the lazier, kindlier forms of debauchery, nor did their social class provide them with periodic outlets for aggression and desire such as country people could find. They were full of revenge and hatred, but in the 'age of enlightenment' it could not be acknowledged that one might have unconscious, uncontrollable desires. The Greeks attributed these to divine possession and got on terms with them. The eighteenth century pretended they did not exist, and therefore the unacknow-ledged impulses turned against the usual symbol of irrational and powerful emotions – women. There was a quite clear need not simply to satisfy lust but to hurt, humiliate and destroy women in order to prove one's potency, even one's existence. The 'normal' trade in women was bad enough, but even this was not sufficient. It was more satisfying to seduce a 'respectable' girl. Narcotics were sometimes used in kidnapping, but often the girls were captured by sheer force. The victim's resistance to the ensuing rape, her cries of fear and pain, were all – quite explicitly, as contemporary erotic books show – valued as part of the achievement. She was then abandoned, and if she was pregnant there was little future for her except in a life of prostitution, since the society that produced these boys and men was also – less openly – engaged in punishing its own irrational needs in the persons of the women who served them. The 'fallen' woman was an object of loathing and contempt to the society that countenanced – even expected – the sexual attitudes that brought about her fall. It is hardly surprising that the tougher women of the lower classes retaliated by making a profit out of the men whenever they could. *The Beggar's Opera* shows Polly's parents shocked at her marriage to Macheath, and her evident love for him; the proper thing for a girl in her situation is to get as much out of her lover as possible, including the price of betraying him to the magistrates, and if she does marry she should make sure she is widowed as soon as possible, with the money in her keeping. *The Beggar's Opera* is funny and light-hearted, but the underlying assumption is that there must be ruthless enmity between the sexes, who cheat, exploit and destroy each other whenever opportunity offers.

Even in 'polite' society this was the rule, though hostilities were conducted in a more graceful manner. It was 'not done' for husband and wife to love each other. A wife of the *beau-monde* was not sexually exploited by her husband for pleasure, but only for breeding. She usually found the means to repay him. Hogarth's series on 'Marriage à la Mode' is ruthlessly revealing of the vicious boredom of such a marriage.

After all this it seems ridiculous to ask whether love was likely to thrive in such as atmosphere. Yet the answer is not the complete negative we might expect. The whole tendency of sexual mores was against the development of anything we might want to call love, but love happened. In *Fanny Hill*, for instance, the touching devotion of Fanny's first lover is emphasized, and he continues faithful until they are finally reunited. This may have been a concession to the sentimental romanticism that was already beginning (in a sense had never ceased) to infiltrate literature but it does show that the writer either approved of this fidelity, or at least thought that his readers would. Another of the oddities of the time is the way fashionable people looked nostalgically to an idealized version of country life, in which the humble tillers of the soil were supposed to display those virtues of innocence, fidelity and domestic content which were so brutally absent from their own. People flocked to hear Arne's ballad opera *Love in a Village*; painters like Morland depicted (and engravers made cheaply available) scenes of rural romance and felicity, of pure maidens and blushing swains, of domestic devotion in a cottage. These same pure maidens, once captured and used by some groups of upper class boys, would be treated with the utmost callousness by the people who admired the pictures and stories. But this double-think itself witnesses to the nostalgia which demanded at least a fantasy of love.

The 'romantic' attitude to sex broke surface towards the end of the eighteenth century and flourished during the early decades of the nineteenth. In an emasculated and more sentimental form it survived throughout the century and still dictates many of our attitudes. But by now it is well mixed, in a combination which is sometimes bafflingly contradictory, with the exploitative attitude, an 'abridged version' of the sacramental attitude, and a nostalgia for the earthy, 'pragmatic' approach which, in fact, does not happen except among groups of young people freed from economic pressures or parental influence. Even then it is usually 'sex in the head', not in Lawrence's sense but in a more pathetic and idealistic sense, trying hard to persuade itself of an attitude of relaxed 'naturalness' about sex which it doesn't really have. So you get a society in which strong sexual desire (passion) is regarded as of overmastering importance, and as constituting a sufficient reason for rejection of any legal or personal obligations that might interfere. But the passion may be short-lived, and its end on one side justifies the ending of the relationship, whatever the feelings of the other person concerned. In other words, the doctrine of romantic passion is being used as a means of exploitation, 'justifying' and 'humanizing' the exploitation for the sake of a type of exploiter less single-minded than some of his predecessors. The sacramental idea is also used to justify exploitation, but it also enters into a more sensitive version of the romantic attitude. Sex as a religion (founded by Lawrence who, like many founders, would have been astounded at the doctrinal development of his creed) appeals to a lot of reasonably comfortable and educated people. Those who are poor, or belong to a working-class culture, take their sex in a more direct way, and although there is an admixture of romance of a rather Victorian variety, and an injection of something inarticulately approaching the sacramental idea via singers like Bob Dylan, the usual mixture is of the pragmatic and the exploitative, with the latter in the ascendant. A conscious sexual 'sacramentalism' is now a middle-class intellectual game, and the word has to be in inverted commas because the communion which is sought and praised is not communion with the divine but with the sexual partner at a deeper level of personality, and also with the deeper reaches of one's own personality.

This extraordinary modern mixture can be roughly paralleled in the Roman Empire, when a similar convergence of different cultures had occurred. But one element makes our situation different, and that is the great influence of the romantic attitude. The nearest approach to this in the ancient world had been the cultivation of sexual but unconsummated relationships between boys and men in Greece, but since these were exclusively male relationships they could not affect the climate of feeling about heterosexual relations, especially married ones. The later European form of romantic sexuality was mainly heterosexual, though sometimes with a homosexual 'feel' to it, and this is the reason why it had a lasting effect on general social attitudes, and eventually on attitudes to marriage itself, throughout western culture.

But originally romance had nothing whatever to do with marriage, in fact marriage was quite incompatible with romantic love. There are wide divergences of opinion about the origins of the Romance doctrines of the thirteenth and fourteenth centuries, and part of the difficulty of establishing them lies in deciding what we mean by 'origins'. These doctrines did not appear fully developed – no theology or ideology ever does. They were not even imported in a recognizably similar form from some other culture, as the Romans imported the cult of Isis more or less ready-made. De Rougement, in *Passion and Society* (a book which time has to a great extent justified against its critics) draws attention to the outbreak of spiritual poetry employing erotic imagery and a dualist, gnostic type of theology, in Mohammedan Arabia of the ninth to twelfth centuries. It shows many resemblances to the Romance poetry of Europe. The doctrine they display is markedly similar to that which is more familiar to Europe in the form of the Manichean heresy, whose medieval form was Catharism. There are thematic links with Persian mysticism and Zoroaster. The orthodox Muslim faith would have none of these doctrines and persecuted them, as the Catholic church persecuted the Cathars. Was there a direct conscious link between the Arab poets and the troubadours? Were the troubadours actually Catharist in belief? For that matter, did the Cathars recognize the eastern origin of their doctrines? It is impossible to be sure, but even if there were some kind of conscious link a new cultural influence of such power does not occur because a group of people latch on to a new doctrine and follow it, unless their own culture is already predisposed to accept it, as I suggested in the last chapter. And if the doctrine expresses a widespread feeling then the chances are this feeling will 'break surface' in explicit form at some point, without any help from outside. When it does so, the doctrine newly formulated will naturally be very like any 'foreign' doctrine which articulates similar needs and hopes. But it is also likely that if individuals do 'import' such doctrine, at the right moment, it will be immediately and widely 'recognized' because it is saying what deeply needs to be said. So whether there was a conscious link, or virtually none, between the Persian mystics, the Arab poets, the Manicheans, the Cathars and the troubadours, all were part of the same movement of thought, and it is thus linked to certain moods of Indian philosophy and erotic religious art. Nor were the opponents of the movement exempt from its effects. The Church persecuted the Cathars and denounced the doctrines of courtly love, but these represented too real a craving for 'something further' in a culture that was brutally materialistic and callous in the operation of power in Church and State, and combined intellectualism and superstition in its religion. In the end the 'new' doctrines came out on top. All European Christianity, Catholic and Protestant, from that time on was dyed in the romantic mood, both in its good and its bad aspects; literature, with the whole climate of thought about sex, was turned into a new channel which it followed (though sometimes underground) from that time onwards. This movement seems to be of a different kind, therefore, from the other 'appreciative' sexual attitudes. It is linked with a wider range of human aspirations and emotions, it does not seem to be merely a reaction or an auxiliary to, or an outlet for, a particular type of social structure, since it assumes so many forms and continues through so many social changes. It is, of course, sociologically 'determined' if we mean by that that it will only occur when social conditions favour it, but it does not serve a straightforward social purpose, indeed it tends to be socially disruptive and anarchic by nature. Its emphasis is on individual experience, yet it can alter the whole nature of a society.

What is the nature of the doctrine?

The description of courtly love is simple in one way because it is so well documented by its own members. But it varied a good deal in practice, as the practice of any faith is bound to do; also its propagandists were constrained both by opposition and by that sense of the arcane which is inherent in the doctrine to be secretive about the exact nature of their doctrine. They used allegory extensively and elaborately, and their meaning is sufficiently far from plain to have kept scholars at a high pitch of quarrelsomeness about it for centuries. Since so much has been written about it I shall not attempt to discuss the obscurities in detail, or do more than outline the most generally accepted version of what courtly love involved.

The cult was essentially the exaltation of unrequited sexual passion. The actual desire, the hopes and fears and the physical stress were important elements. The 'lady' chosen by a knight was to be served as if she had been a goddess. Her lightest word was law, absolute faithfulness was demanded. (This did not, incidentally, rule out sexual intercourse with lower-class women, in the true 'exploitative' tradition!) Devoted service might earn her favour, the privilege of a kiss, of caressing her naked body and even of spending the night with her, but in the 'extreme' romance tradition intercourse was forbidden. This is not as odd as it seems because satisfied desire gradually changes the character of the relationship, and the couple cease to be 'romantic' though they may remain devoted. This cult saw sexual passion as a spiritually liberating thing, freeing love from the 'earthiness' of normal, orthodox sex. This shows the links with Catharism and similar doctrines which rejected sex in order to liberate the spirit. However, in some versions the relationship does appear to be consummated, but its passionate character is preserved by the risky situation involved, the need for secrecy, the desperate planning, the frequent partings. The enemy, as before, is 'orthodox' sex, in marriage, in which there are no longer any obstacles to union, therefore (according to this doctrine) no yearning towards spiritual freedom, which must have obstacles to overcome if it is to continue unabated. The 'lady' was therefore never one's wife, though she was often (usually, in fact) someone else's wife. The husband did not necessarily object. He probably had a 'lady' of his own! Sex in marriage was a distasteful necessity to the true disciple of 'courtesy', but a landowner must have children. The whole set-up is full of delicate paradoxes, and the elaborate rules, and 'courts of love' organized among the French aristocracy to sort out 'crimes' against love show how this obscurity, complexity and ambiguity were part of the whole atmosphere of an esoteric doctrine which only an élite could understand and fully live, though the more carnal minded might absorb similar attitudes. In this also there is a reflection of the Catharist Church in which only the inner circle of 'Christians' (whom the Inquisitors sarcastically called the 'Perfect') who had received the sacrament of the *consolamentum* were expected to live according to the full rigour of the doctrine, entirely without sex, in poverty and privation. The 'believers' accepted the doctrine but were not expected to conform to it. In practice this meant that 'believers' had a good deal of sexual licence, since according to the gnostic beliefs sex was evil anyway, being married made it no better, and procreation was the worst evil of all. The inquisitors, of course, made it all sound much worse than it probably was. There are recorded cases of devotion and deep, sincere love among these people which moved even so implacable an enemy as St Bernard to commend the purity of their morals. Here again we have that hopeful and persistent human phenomenon – the power of love – which we recognize so clearly, yet can so ill define.

The love poems of Wolfram von Eschenbach are in the full romance tradition, yet there is nothing of the feverish, brooding intensity of the 'full' romance doctrine in them. There is rather a delicate, joyful, intensely human recognition of the beauty of sexual love. And among the Cathars, whose extreme doctrine could culminate in the ecstatic suicide by fasting of the 'Endura', there were these glowing examples of brotherly love and generosity to the poor, a kind of love with an outward-turning amplitude which contradicts the essentially 'interior' gnostic doctrines. Love finds its way round corners and through underground passages and emerges, somehow, somewhere, though usually with little acclaim. It is perhaps useful to notice that several of the troubadours were known to be homosexual, and that the lady was sometimes addressed (especially in Spain, as well as by the Arab Romance poets) by masculine titles. De Rougemont explains this by saying that 'the narcissism inherent in any so-called "Platonic" love involves on the sexual plane obvious deviations into which it would be difficult to deny that some troubadours were tempted'. This may be so, but we should also notice that homosexuals are often people who are more than usually sensitive, and therefore more than usually repelled by the degraded nature (which is often real but may be imaginary) of heterosexual relations. The same almost 'instinctive' revulsion from the brutal commercialism, the exploitation, the *impersonal* quality of virtually all 'orthodox' sex (legal or otherwise, recognized by the Church or not) which drove people to look for a more human and 'spiritual' love between the sexes, would also encourage the development of homosexual relationships, carnal or not, since these did not enter into the normal, accepted, sexual 'scene' and were therefore not (it might seem) corrupted by it.

This brief glance at the doctrine of romantic love as it developed in Europe in its first ascendancy is clearly inadequate and passes over a number of important questions. Since to do even scant justice to the Romance movement in these pages would unbalance the structure of a book such as this I can only beg the reader's indulgence.

But why should such a thing have occurred, and spread, and assumed such strange and varied forms, and endured so obstinately? I would like to suggest an answer which ties up with some of the things I said about the emergence of a notion of mature sexual love in Shakespeare and which was again submerged by other forces, until a much later time. I suggested that the anti-sexual feeling of the Middle Ages actually helped to develop the sense of individual selfhood, in fact the possibility of a *personal* love, which at first could only be thought of *apart* from sex. This chapter has perhaps helped to show why it could only develop in separation from the sexual context.

The romance doctrines had their roots in eastern mysticism, in the doctrines of liberation from the illusory emotions and concerns of the body. The dualist way of expressing this made the aim of the movement of liberation quite clear – it was the 'real' 'spiritual' self that was to be set free, not some half-alive ghost which would survive in the depressing 'underworld' life of middle-eastern and Greek mythologies. I cannot see how, without this forceful concept of the evil body and the good spirit which was to be freed, the human aspiration for completeness and reality could have taken hold of people's minds and hearts. Dualism led to frightful aberrations and distortions, but it transformed the notion of human selfhood from something earth-bound, rationally controlled and basically pessimistic (with periods of irrational madness which had to be allowed for) to an assertive, future-orientated concept of a life capable of radical transformation and glorification. The original Christian notion had been of the radical transformation of the whole spiritual physical being, but this simply did not catch on, and was altered in the way I described. It is only now being re-discovered. Meanwhile the Christian world 'carried' (rather than taught) the aspiring, self-discovering, gnostic ideas. But the Romance doctrines developed (still by rejection of sex in the normal sense) a role for bodily feelings and bodily beauty which was truly a personal one, and something approaching a whole relationship. The 'everydayness' of marriage and procreation was unthinkable in this relationship, because of their identification with what the troubadours considered to be the iniquitous bonds of a loveless, impersonal lust. Romantic love rejected lust, in or out of marriage, as the enemy of 'true' love, and it also rejected ordinary law and custom which treated people as non-persons and obliged them to be and do things that were destructive to their spiritual knowledge and selfhood. Those who proclaimed it, the troubadours and minnesingers, were themselves symbols of spiritual freedom. They were often bachelors, or at least sat easy to their marriages. They were also either landless or quite uninterested in the land from which their living came. They were sometimes very poor. In Germany some of the minnesingers were 'Dienstmänner' or landless knights. They had titles but were virtually serfs since they depended on some Lord for their livelihood, lacking the only source of knightly independence – land. They were despised by the landed nobility, but sometimes achieved positions of power and influence by sheer brains and opportunism. Others took to a wandering life and went from castle to castle, welcomed as singers and story-tellers. They, and the troubadours, were therefore not integrated into the power structure of society. They were natural rebels and prophets and their social criticism was sometimes scathing and got them into trouble. In this respect also the whole Romance movement was anti-establishment.

We have therefore a movement whose roots are strongly mystical, whose validity can only be underwritten by personal experience, which stresses the possibility of transcendence and spiritual achievement for human beings *as individuals*, which sees bodily emotions as vital in this context, but also sees them as discovered *in love* – in a true, personal relationship of a close, trusting and faithful kind. What emerges, in the end, is the idea that sexual *love* – not just sex – is an ennobling and spiritually important experience, whereas lust is just about the opposite. And we see the Romance tradition, modified by human experience and by the lost prestige of the aristocracy that practised it, providing the way forward out of the sixteenth-century impasse. The encounter of the anti-sex and anti-woman obsession of the medieval Church, with the Renaissance counter-assertion of the pleasure of the flesh and the rights of man to decide as he wishes in defiance of any god, was unlikely to produce more than a war. The creative leap forward that Shakespeare managed (almost alone, apparently) was made by a recognition of the personalism of the Romance tradition. He brought together the sense of personal value and integrity that the emphasis on virginity had allowed to develop, and he put it in the 'romantic' context of a whole love between persons. He added to this the positive Renaissance valuation of the body and sex, but with a definitely Christian slant – the satisfactions of loving sex are god-given, they are 'blessings', not 'rights'. He thus pulled the romantic tradition into the open and deprived it of its febrile, rootless quality. Passion is there, sexual anguish and loss is there, but these are not ends in themselves. Shakespeare's figures of tragic sexuality – Othello, Leontes, Hamlet – are people who are unable to recognize that sexual *satisfaction* can be a 'spiritual' thing. Just *because* their wives (or Hamlet's mother, or intended bride) are frankly 'at home' with their sexuality, and neither ashamed nor anguished about it, they are suspected. In their eyes, satisfactory sexuality *must* be 'fleshly' and evil. For them, only shame, or the agony of unrequited love can 'purify' sexual feeling. And it seems to me that by stating so clearly the innocence of the suspected women – even Gertrude's guilt is never established as existing outside her son's imagination – Shakespeare is saying what perhaps could not be said in a more direct way, perhaps could not even be directly envisaged: that a truly personal, whole, sexual relationship can exist which involves, and indeed grows by, sexual pleasure and satisfaction. And in that case *married* sex is not only a possible setting for a truly spiritual love, but also the most likely one. Truly, a strange development of the Romance doctrines, but, I think, the most valid and human one. Unfortunately, as with St Paul who had a similar concept of married sexuality, few people were able to grasp such a development. The climate of opinion was not prepared for it, and it disappeared from view. Later versions of the Romance doctrines reverted to the glorification of unsatisfied desire, and felt that consummated love was not quite nice, or at least not very 'romantic', which is true. So the romantic heroes and heroines generally came to an untimely end, thus avoiding the perils of domestic bliss. It may seem odd to set Victorian romantic prudery in among the types of the cultivation of sex, but, historically and psychologically, that is where it belongs. Sexual emotion is just as sexual when unsatisfied, as Shakespeare knew.

IV

LOVE IN FAMILY-TYPE RELATIONSHIPS

THE consideration of sex and sexual love is bound to occupy an important part of the whole in a book on the concept of love. The remaining chapters will show, among other things, that though many aspects and kinds of love must be regarded as non-sexual there is no clear-cut boundary. The varieties in attitudes to sexuality make it clear already that there is no single type of love that can be labelled 'sexual'.

The first chapter examined the way in which methods of upbringing, varied as they may be, seem intent on preventing rather than cultivating the growth of love, and how it kept on breaking out in spite of this. The next two examined a wide range of sexual situations with a view to seeing how love fared in them. In all these cases the presence or absence of love was something that could be observed, but did not necessarily occupy the thoughts or modify the aims and actions of the societies and people concerned. In some cases it did, in others it was not a concept that entered into the situation at all. (It is important to remember that our word 'love' is used to include both *eros* and *agape*. And in the ancient world *eros* meant sexual passion, not love in our sense. Hence the use of the word in the ancient world does not mean that people were thinking about 'love' in the modern sense.) And where it occurred it would often be seen to do so in reaction to, or in spite of, a situation apparently designed to exclude it. From all this, a reasonably clear idea of what we mean by the everyday use of the word 'love' began to emerge. It seemed to be a sentiment, desire or 'drive' that tended to reach beyond the limitations of the given social and personal situation, in an attempt to achieve greater depth or breadth of life experience, and sometimes this was explicitly recognized as a transformation of human life. Between persons, this seemed to mean a growing, many-levelled communication, in which the whole personality was, ideally, involved.

In order to take this definition further I propose to reverse the procedure I have used so far. Instead of examining certain situations and seeing whether and how they are 'loving' or capable of developing a capacity for love, I shall examine certain relationships which are normally, and often explicitly, regarded as loving ones, and see whether they really are loving, in the sense developed so far.

'The family' is the setting which is traditionally and popularly expected to enshrine loving relationships. It is also the natural target of people who recognize that what is labelled 'love' in this setting is frequently nothing of the kind, and who demand, therefore, not more loving family relationships but no family relationships at all. The first chapter showed how virtually all cultures develop a pattern of child rearing apparently designed to suppress, or carefully canalize, love. The distortion of love in the European 'closed' family is naturally the target of contemporary critics.

Here is the opinion of a young psychiatrist, as reported recently in a big Sunday newspaper: He described the bourgeois family unit as 'the ultimate and lethal gas chamber in our society'. Within the family, covert violence took the form of deforming children by the parents' enforcement of their own roles. In the bourgeois family 'the individual is unable to enjoy himself, nor is he enjoyed by anyone else. The individual can escape from the deforming influence of the family, and of family-like institutions, only by learning to enjoy himself, and by acting out his fantasies and dreams to the full'. (This is assumed to be impossible in the bourgeois family.) The alternative proposed was a 'commune' system of living, which he said was best seen at present in Cuba and China, in which the bourgeois family was replaced by the 'extended family'. Within the commune individuals would be able to establish totally free relationships. 'Every individual may then touch anyone anyhow in any way he wants, and learn how not to be tortured by possessiveness or jealousy.' The deforming effect of bourgeois family life would be overcome because children would be given the opportunity to relate freely with people other than their biological parents.

This kind of objection is not new. The word 'love' is not used in this passage, but it is clear that this doctor considers that family life as it is mostly lived in the West prevents love. The capacity to 'enjoy and be enjoyed' is clearly part of his definition of love. The emotional bias, here, has distorted the way the case is presented. The 'bourgeois' family is the kind condemned, and my guess is that this label is applied to families that 'deform' the children by possessiveness or imposed standards, and so on. A family that did not have these effects would thereby be exempt from the 'bourgeois' label whatever its sociological classification. Also the 'commune' idea, far from being new, is one of the oldest known methods of producing a conformist society. There is no evidence whatever that the 'free' relationships thus made are any more loving than those with parents and siblings, and there is overwhelming evidence (overlooked by the opponents of family ties) that children brought up on communitarian lines from birth – even when those who care for them are conscientious and devoted – are noticeably *less* capable of forming relationships of any but the most fleeting and superficial kind.

The outburst quoted is, however, an expression of a genuine revulsion from the way traditional European family relationships have been exploited to bind and confine and, as he said, 'deform' human lives. It is natural that someone brought up in a culture where this kind of thing is common should assume that such deformation only occurs in that culture. The first chapters may have helped to show that the tendency to suppress and 'deform' is in fact virtually universal. But the objector is, if rather angrily, on the side of the angels. He wants people to be free to love, able to 'relate freely'. The fact that the type of upbringing he favours would tend to produce people unable to relate at all is not really relevant.

(In passing, it is relevant to notice that, although the commune experiments in Cuba and China are both too recent and too suspicious of outside observers to provide any reliable evidence about the effects on the children, the similar methods in the Israeli Kibbutzim have shown disturbing results in the emerging adolescents, even though the Kibbutzim have never maintained a complete separation of parents and children. The tendency recently has been to increase the amount of time children spend with their parents.)

There is an assumption behind many expressions of anti-family opinion that whereas, inevitably, everyone is influenced by his environment, some kinds of influence are 'de-forming', whereas others set people 'free'. It is not here a question of deciding that one kind of formation is right and to be preferred (this has been the almost universal assumption behind cultural conditioning both primitive and sophisticated) but that there is some kind of human life-style which is natural, human, proper, 'real', and that this does not need to be formed but rather to be allowed to grow without hindrance. Rousseau was an early exponent of this philosophy, and it has had many adherents, all of them the product of restrictive cultural environments. And if what has been so far noticed is correct there is indeed a vital truth behind this assumption, even though its results in terms of worked-out methods of child-care have been less successful than was hoped. This truth is that love is indeed what might be called the 'real' human activity or drive, which allows the person to develop most completely as himself. The fallacy lies in assuming that the removal of (possibly) deforming influences will allow this human reality to grow unhampered. Almost the reverse is the case, in that even bad and disturbed relationships in childhood give more chance of developing a capacity for love later than the *absence* of any long-term relationships. The outlook is poor in both cases but the point is that what has grown crooked may possibly be straightened, or even be developed in its crooked state, but what has never received enough nourishment to grow at all simply isn't there to develop.

The most sensitive accounts of human relationships are generally fictional. I have therefore picked out some well-known examples of relationships in novels, to show how loving relationships, even when 'loving' has to go in inverted commas, do in fact develop the capacity to love although they may be far from ideal as relationships.

My first example has become a cliché. It is a period cliché which shows the ideal of the relationship between mother and son which was accepted by a whole era. *Little Lord Fauntleroy* is a classic tear-jerker about the devoted love of a little boy for his young, widowed mother. When the family lawyer brings to the young American widow the news that her son is now the heir to the earldom of her dead husband's father (his older brothers having died) her reaction is a rich field for would-be Freudian speculation:

'Oh', she said, 'will he have to be taken away from me? We love each other so much! He is such a happiness to me! He is all I have. I have tried to be a good mother to him.' And her sweet young voice trembled, and the tears rushed to her eyes. 'You do not know what he has been to me!' she said.

During the voyage to England the child hears that he is not

to live with his mother when he reaches his new home – this is because of the old Earl's prejudice against his dead son's American wife, whom he refuses to have in his home, but the child is not told the reason. 'When he learned of the coming separation his grief was so great that Mr Havisham saw that the Earl had been wise in making the arrangement that his mother should be quite near him, and see him often.' On his first day at the castle he hears that he now owns a pony – a dream come true – and is asked by the Earl if he would like to go and see it at once:

> Fauntleroy drew a long breath, 'I *want* to see it', he said. 'I want to see it so much I can hardly wait. But I'm afraid there isn't much time.'
> 'You *must* go and see your mother this afternoon?' asked the Earl. 'You think you can't put it off?'
> 'Why', said Fauntleroy, 'she has been thinking about me all the morning, and I have been thinking about her.'

The evening before, in his first conversation with his grandfather, he shows the Earl his locket with a picture of his mother, whom he calls 'Dearest':

> 'I suppose you think you are very fond of her?' the Earl said.
> 'Yes', answered Lord Fauntleroy, in a gentle tone, and with simple directness, 'I do think so and I think it's true. You see, Mr. Hobbs was my friend, and Dick and Bridget and Mary and Michael, they were my friends too; but Dearest – well she is my *close* friend, and we always tell each other everything. My father left her to me to take care of, and when I am a man I am going to work and earn money for her.'

Here is the bourgeois family ideal without even the variation of relationships provided by two parents and several brothers and sisters. The mother and son relationship is

explicitly described as close, deep and very emotional. They
are almost like lovers. This intensity is scarcely ideal from the
point of view of ordinary mental health, even without
inevitable suspicions about the overtones of incest. But the
author had no such worries. She considered the relationship
natural, beautiful, and also exemplary and she expected her
readers to take the same view, and they did. But the really
interesting point is the attitudes to other people which she
described in the little boy. She clearly regarded these as the
ones one would expect as a result of this type of very intimate
love between mother and son. The child is first introduced to
the reader in company with the local grocer, to whom he is
confiding the disturbing news about his change of fortunes.
He is shown in close and cordial relationship with a number of
trades-people in the area, as well as with other boys. These
relationships display a deeply personal quality, there is a real
sympathy, a quick response to another's troubles, and an
immense and uninhibited pleasure in being able to help.
His approach to strangers, including his fierce and awe-
inspiring grandfather, is relaxed and without shyness or fear.
He expects to be liked, because he likes people and it hasn't
occurred to him that they might not return the compliment.
He has a great capacity for enjoyment of things and people
and others clearly find him a source of enjoyment, at all sorts
of levels.

Here is a child, who, in the author's opinion, is supremely
capable of forming 'free relationships with people other than
his biological parents', of 'enjoying and being enjoyed', as a
direct result of a very close and intense relationship with his
mother. Is this credible or has the author falsified the psychological probabilities? Certainly the two of them are idealized:
the mother is invariably sweet and patient, Cedric is never
rude, silly or out of temper. But Cedric's sense of responsibility for his mother is a real burden, and it clearly *does*

'deform' to some extent though the author did not think of it that way. This child *is* inhibited and constrained by the nature of his unnaturally unique bond with this mother. And yet it does not seem odd that this too intense relationship should, in practice, set the child free to encounter others openly and fearlessly, to discover the world and work out his problems creatively. It does not seem odd because what is described as a loving relationship clearly *is* a loving relationship, even though there are elements in it that tend to distort. And the real love is what counts. Mrs. Hodgson Burnett's book appealed to its first readers, and still appeals to so many that it continues to go into edition after edition, because in spite of the outdated class-feeling, the sentimental vocabulary, the incredible 'goodness' of Cedric, he somehow rings true. This *is* how love affects people. In a sense it is wishful thinking, as the critics assert. Little boys, however much loved, are not as good as Cedric, nor can problems always be solved by sheer goodness and love, but the popular instinct that continues to value the story is more discerning than a culture suspicious of love is inclined to admit. It is not necessary to underwrite the possessiveness, the fears, the jealousies, the restrictions of the 'bourgeois' family in order to recognize that love can and does happen in it, and that it works, not because it is bourgeois but because it is loving – and it is loving in spite of all the other things, for love can co-exist with all the bourgeois vices, as it can with sexual repression or even exploitation. It may be restricted and stunted, but it is there, or at least it can be. It is perhaps worth noting that 'Lord Fauntleroy' was based on a real child, the author's own son, so maybe she knew what she was talking about.

One of the most famous of all fictional children is David Copperfield, and he is almost a text-book case. Cared for in early childhood by a doting but weak and silly widowed mother, and the sturdy servant Peggotty, he is spontaneously affectionate when he gets a chance, but his loves are not 'earthed' by everyday practicalities. They are the loves of a child whose parental ties are deeply felt but not established in the routines of a many-sided, practical relationship. The beloved servant, Peggotty, down to earth as she is, lives a servant's life, close and trusted but not providing a 'model' by which David can work out his own attitudes to others. His childish passion for the entrancing 'little Emily' has this fairy-tale quality.

> Of course I was in love with little Emily. I am sure I loved that baby quite as truly, quite as tenderly, with greater purity and disinterestedness, than can enter into the best love of a later time of life, high and ennobling as it is. I am sure my fancy raised up something around that blue-eyed mite of a child, which etherialized, and made a very angel of her.

Lacking the security of a family love with firm roots in daily life, that is all he can do with his beloved. The brutality of his stepfather, the calculated cruelty of his school, the lack of any sense of support or care at home after his mother's second marriage make any development in the ability to love unlikely. At school he develops a passion for Steerforth, a vain, ruthlessly selfish boy whom he idealizes also, because that is the only way he can love. The shock of his mother's death, and that of her new baby, reinforces this tendency. He cannot cope with the memory of her more recent life: her cowardice in withholding her love from him for fear of her husband, her failure to support him against that unspeakable stepfather, her general pathetic weakness of character. These he cannot admit, because such failures are incompatible with the only kind of love of which he is capable.

> From the moment of my knowing of the death of my mother, the idea of her as she had been of late had vanished from me. I remembered her, from that instant, only as the

young mother of my earliest impressions, who had been used to wind her bright curls round and round her finger, and dance with me at twilight in the parlour. What Peggotty had told me now, was so far from bringing me back to the later period, that it rooted the earlier image in my mind. It may be curious, but it is true. In her death she winged her way back to her calm untroubled youth, and cancelled all the rest. The mother who lay in the grave was the mother of my infancy; the little creature in her arms was myself, as I had once been, hushed for ever on her bosom.

When, eventually, he encounters a real and sturdy love in his aunt, Miss Trotwood, he cannot take it in. Greatly as he appreciates and reveres her, and manages to discern her real feelings at odd moments, he is constantly disconcerted by her abrupt, awkward manner, her undemonstrative behaviour. He finds a security in her, but cannot open out towards her. And he marries a silly, weak little creature as like his mother as makes no difference, for the only kind of love he can manage is the worship of an 'angelic', almost disembodied creature. That Dora is a vain little goose, childishly selfish and as unable to develop a mature love as her husband, is all too apparent to everyone except David. Yet she *does* love him, in her feeble, demanding way, and her clinging need brings out whatever there is in David of courage and patience. At first all his effort goes into trying to make Dora into something she isn't and can't be. He loves her, but his love still cannot cope with imperfection. He is irritated by her, because she cannot be what she *has* to be, if he is to love her. The irritation betrays his fear of facing reality. She *must* be perfect. When he cannot avoid recognizing her weaknesses he sets himself to love her all the same but, by 'preserving' her, untouched, like a pretty bird. In the end it is Dora, not David, who is the realist. In the face of death, silly Dora has more self-knowledge than her husband can bear to corroborate:

'I am afraid, dear, I was too young. I don't mean in years
only, but in experience, and thoughts and everything. I was
such a silly little creature! I am afraid it would have been
better if we had only loved each other as boy and girl, and
forgotten it. I have begun to think I was not fit to be a
wife.'

I try to stay my tears, and to reply, 'Oh Dora, love, as fit
as I to be husband.'

'I don't know', with the old shake of her curls. 'Perhaps!
But if I had been more fit to be married, I might have made
you more so, too . . . as years went on, my dear boy would
have wearied of his child wife. . . . He would have been
more and more sensible of what was wanting in his home.
. . . It is better as it is.'

'Oh Dora, dearest, dearest, do not speak to me so.
Every word seems a reproach!'

'No, not a syllable', she answers, kissing me. 'Oh my dear,
you never deserved it, and I loved you far too well to say a
reproachful word to you, in earnest – it was all the merit I
had, except being pretty – or you thought me so.'

Here is about as unsatisfactory a marriage as one could find,
and the reasons are clear. Yet Dickens shows that these two
did love each other, in their desperately inadequate way.
With everything in their upbringing – not to mention the
prudish romantic ethos of the time – against them, they are
shown developing spiritually through this experience. Dora,
as she says, 'wouldn't have improved' in respect of sense and
dependability. But her love teaches her the courage to
recognize her own failure, and *accept* it *herself*, not lay the
blame on David. As for David, the loss of Dora shakes him
to the foundations, because it finally destroys his carefully
nurtured fantasy-love which can no longer survive either in
the form of an angel to be worshipped or a frail treasure to be
enclosed and protected. In the end, he discovers a different
love, and his marriage to the grave and serene Agnes, though

it stretches one's credulity a little, is in keeping with the rest, for if such a boy were ever to grow out of the fantasy-love which was all he learned as a child he would need to start over again, with a new 'mother'. This is Agnes' role.

The Brown family in *National Velvet* are as bourgeois as can be, though very much of the *petit* variety. Their family life is a close network of bubbling emotions, which are meticulously and hilariously described. Here is fourteen-year old, boy-like, intense, horse-mad Velvet, talking to her vastly fat, ex-channel swimming, dominating, looming mother, as she does up her mother's petticoat one evening.

'S'awful to grow up,' said Velvet.

'Nope,' said Mrs Brown.

'Why isn't it?'

'Things come suitable to the time,' said Mrs Brown.

The thin slip, the quivering twig, looked back at her mother.

'Lot o' nonsense,' said Mrs Brown, 'talked about growing up'. She stepped into her princess petticoat and drew it up. 'Tie me', she said. The candle in the red candlestick drowned itself in fat and went out. 'Childbirth', said the voice, gruff and soothing, talking to the star and to the child (and the child knelt at the strings of the petticoat), 'an' being in love. An' death. You can't know 'em till you come to 'em. No use guessing and dreading. You kin call it pain ... but what's pain? Depends on who you are an' how you take it. Tie that bottom string looser. Don't you dread nothing, Velvet.'

'But you're so mighty. Like a tree', said Velvet.

'Shivery to be your age. You don't know nothin'. Later on you get coated over.... You don't change nothin' underneath.'

'All the same it's awful to grow up,' said Velvet. 'All this changing and changing, an' got to be ready for something. I don't ever want children. Only horses.'

'Who can tell?' said Mrs Brown.

'I've got Me', said Velvet, putting her thin hand across her breast, 'I can't ever be anything else but Me.'

'You're all safe,' said Mrs Brown carelessly, stooping with grunts to pull up her dress. 'You got both of us, you *an'* me. Say your prayers now an' get along.'

'Not yet, not yet.'

'Say your prayers, I say. Down on your knees an' say your prayers. You go plunging off this time o' night, don't you? Getting into your bed all of a daze an' a worry. Say your prayers, I say!'

Velvet went on her knees in the middle of the floor.

A mother-goddess incarnate, Mrs Brown is the type of woman who can crush and cripple her children with terrible ease. But Velvet's passion for her is an emotion whose context, clearly, is a loving relationship. The power and ruthlessness do 'deform', in a sense, but they also comfort, support and give courage. So Velvet obstinately overcomes one apparently insurmountable obstacle after another in the crazy project which she engages in almost by accident. Fearful, tense with nerves, she perseveres, and in the magnificent climax of the book (which is somehow entirely credible) wins the Grand National on her own horse. She does this entirely on her own initiative; her mother, instead of swallowing her, has set her free to achieve. When Mrs Brown gets the news, through the press, she goes to the hospital where Velvet, brought there after she fainted from nervous strain and exhaustion, is waking from the effects of a sleeping draught:

In the morning at the Liverpool Central mother sat by Velvet's bed (mother, carrying her washing things in her old 'Art' bag).

'I've come to take you home, dearie,' she said.

Velvet, dazed with her sleep, still, and brilliantly happy, smiled through her dreams.

'Nice kettle of fish,' said Mrs Brown.

'Travelled up through the night,' said mother. 'You done well, Velvet.'

This was the summit, and Velvet felt the beating of glory.

It is because of this huge, dangerous mother, the perfect example of the type of maternal influence most feared by psychiatrists, that Velvet emerges from the glory and the publicity and the flattery, unscathed and still able to grow:

> Chrysanthemums, roses in winter, glacéd sweets, love letters, interviews, satin pillow-dolls – the house had flowed with gifts. Edwina, Mally, and Merry had eaten themselves sick, but Velvet, who did not care for flowers, could not stomach many sweets, did not read the love letters, never played with dolls, remained with her real desires sharp and intact, the ascending spirit with which she was threaded unquenched by surfeit.

The curious thing about this 'super daydream' as one critic called it, is that its wholly incredible coincidences, strokes of good fortune, and final triumph, are believable, within its cover, *because* of the brilliantly observed quality of the personal relationship. Adolescent girls are highly unlikely to win the Grand National, but we recognize the spirit that can compass that kind of achievement emerging with beautiful emotional logic from the quality of the love between mother and daughter. Mrs Brown *loves* her nervous, over-sensitive child, and love sets her free. One may wonder what kind of a grown woman Velvet would become. Would she be able to mature sexually? Maybe not, given the type of person her mother is. But if the relationship deforms, the love present in it liberates. Sexually 'normal' or not, Velvet is set to be a remarkable human being.

It is no coincidence that two of the books from which I

have quoted so far are children's books, and that the other is Victorian (as is one of the children's books). Children's books continue even now to present satisfactory family relationships, though there has been a recent crop of books that reacted against this by putting families in the background and stressing 'gang-relationships'. This tradition of books about children on their own began in earnest with E. Nesbit, and Arthur Ransome founded it even more firmly. Although the parents in the background are generally 'nice people' there are clear admissions that confidence is not always complete and that one is sometimes better off away from the ignorance, prejudice, and general lack of understanding of parents. A few generations earlier it would have been unthinkable to suggest the imperfection of parents. In Mrs Molesworth's earlier work, for instance, it is 'poor little London street boys' only who might be supposed to have imperfect parents, but later she portrays clearly the limitations of parental (or at least paternal) understanding, though she does her best to make this tolerable to the child-reader by explaining the inevitable remoteness of fathers from children's concerns and motives. The scene in *Carrots* in which his father has him shut up in a closet as a self-confessed liar and thief because his childish ignorance has involved him in a muddle of mis-statements and contradictions is almost unbearable. Yet the assumption, in children's books and in Dickens and even in Jane Austen for all her ruthless perceptiveness, is that, although family relationships may be brutal or miserable or estranged or possessive, or merely formal, they *can* be truly loving. Elizabeth Bennet's affection for her father in *Pride and Prejudice* is as real as it is realistic. Mr. Wickfield's love for his daughter Agnes, in *David Copperfield*, is morbid and possessive but genuine, and she is not damaged, though she is unhappy. Even Uriah Heep and his mother are portrayed as held together by a real bond of love, loathsome as they both are in every other respect. In *Fathers and Sons* Turgenev shows two fathers who dote on their sons and are terrified of alienating them – which they successfully do, precisely through this lack of self-confidence, and of the directness and intimacy that confidence might have made possible. Yet even the repulsive and destructive Bazarov cannot be as nihilist as he would like, and his love for his parents, grudging and disdainful as it is has created in him a capacity for emotional response which he rejects in theory and fears in practice. Dying, he admits that his twittery, ignorant, adoring, irritating, pathetic parents have a quality not to be found in the world in which he himself had made his life. To the woman who visits him in his sickness, for whom he had developed a reluctant passion, he says:

> I daresay my father will tell you what a man is being lost to Russia, but that is all rubbish. Nevertheless, do not undeceive him, for he is old, old. Rather, comfort him as you would comfort a child, and also be kind to my mother. Two such mortals as them you will not find in all *your* great world....'

Over and over again, in novels and stories from the most naïve to the most sophisticated, the nineteenth century acknowledged the reality of the love to be found in family relationships. The nineteenth century is the crucial period for the development of this sentiment, because it was at this time that family ties in all classes (for different reasons) were becoming less a matter of economic or dynastic usefulness (entailing a sense of obligation, and respect, and loyalty, but not necessarily anything more intimate) and were coming to depend for their continuance mainly on emotional ties. This new awareness of the emotional quality of family relationships developed, as well as recognized, the sense of the primary importance of family ties, and created the climate of thought in which it seemed wrong even to think that children should *not* love their parents, or that parents should not always be right.

This enforced hypocrisy, which became so prevalent, arose from the fear that without the emotional bond of family love the social structure would crumble, as indeed it would have done, and in time did do. It was this virtual enforcement of close ties, and a pretended love where no real love existed, that finally led people like Samuel Butler to reject the whole notion of family love as nothing but a means of oppression and distortion. He has had many followers. It has become the new cliché, replacing the old ones of family love, that family ties are more likely to be destructive than not. It is surprising how few people stop to notice whether they actually are, or to wonder why so many children of possessive mothers, or crude and insensitive fathers, grow up able to love *at all*, though maybe with quite a few kinks of their own. The need to break out of the nineteenth-century mould, and therefore to break down its assumptions and pretences, led to the analysis of family relationships by Freud, and his description of what goes wrong. The misleading assumption has been that *how* a relationship goes wrong is the *reason* it goes wrong. An unresolved Oedipal conflict is one way of describing the development of one kind of adult neurosis, but it avoids the question why among boys who are emotionally clamped to Mum some grow up bitter, withdrawn, and unable to form satisfactory relationships with women, while others, though they have difficulties traceable to this cause, do manage to love and to marry and to work through the difficulties and bring up reasonably stable children. The answer could be the simple one that some possessive mothers love their sons, and others don't.

An extension of this answer will be the equally simple fact that some of these men meet and marry women who love them, and others either don't encounter a woman who can love them, or don't marry her, or marry an unloving woman. For one of the few facts about emotional development that has been established by overwhelming evidence is that a child who is loved, even in very poor financial and psychological circumstances, has a good chance to learn to love in turn; also (though the evidence for this is inevitably more equivocal) that a child deprived of love can to some extent 'begin over again' at a later age, if someone loves him enough to let him 'begin again' and not demand a maturity of response which is, in practice, impossible. The reason why fostering of deprived children is often less successful than, in theory, it should be, is that few foster parents realize that a 'deprived' child may need to 'begin again' in slowly establishing the trust and confidence he has never been able to learn before. He must be allowed to be a baby, and normally people can't take this from a 'big' boy or girl. But there is evidence that the thing can be done. One extreme case demonstrated this, when an autistic child of about nine, with no capacity whatever for relating to others, was gradually brought back to something approaching emotional normality by a woman psychiatrist, who allowed him to regress even to the pre-natal stage, to curl up against her in a foetal position, and – at his own pace – to 'begin again' from there, learning little by little the confidence of the baby in his mother's care and constancy. She loved him enough to do this, and love is the accurate description of what is involved in such an act of continuing self-giving, backed by hope and vision enough to make sense of it.

This psychiatrist was, in the usual jargon, the 'mother figure'. Less dramatically many a wife has done the same service for an emotionally immature husband, many a husband for a childish wife. It has been done by lovers and in all sorts of non-sexual relationships also. Sometimes the person later becomes capable of an 'equal' relationship with the one who helped, sometimes he or she goes on to someone else to find equality.

It is usual, and I have done it myself, to refer to people who assist this late emotional growth (or who do it in childhood for those deprived of parents) as substitute mothers or fathers. This is usefully descriptive, but it should perhaps be made clear that these titles are arbitrary. The mother, or father, and any others who may assist the growth of love, are all doing the same work of love. Parents are the usual people to do it, but strictly speaking one might just as well say that a particular mother was a substitute wife or sister as that a particular wife or sister was a substitute mother, if any of these gave the essential service of helping the growth from desiring, dependent, acceptance *of* love to generous self-giving *in* love.

Jane Eyre is an extraordinary torrent of gothic-romantic emotions of various kinds, and among the points Charlotte Brontë was making a lesson on the deforming effects of the early deprivation of love was not a conscious intention. But one of the obvious things about her heroine is that although she is passionate, and longs to love, she is also suspicious of love, plays with it dangerously, uses it, and also is doubtful of its possibility. She makes a catastrophic mess of her romance with Rochester, and her responsibility for this is not concealed by the self-righteous purity of her conscious motives. Yet she is capable of love for her pupil Adèle, as well as for the Byronic hero. Her use of her sexuality is exploitative but not only that. It is, finally, loving, though still possessive and insecure: Rochester in full power was too much for her; Rochester blind and dependent she can cope with. Deformed she certainly is, and probably permanently, but in her deformity she can manage to love. When one looks to the earlier part of the book the roots of this mixture are plain to see. Her early childhood was spent among people who disliked and abused her, and whom she hated. In her final revolt she turns on her aunt Mrs Reed and denounces her: 'You think I have no feelings, and that I can do without one bit of love or kindness; but I cannot live so.' This is not how a child would speak or think, yet it expresses the situation well enough. But she 'cannot live so', and she makes the most of the crumbs of affection that come her way. There is the cross-tempered nurse-maid, Bessie, who is yet fond of her in a rough way, and before she is sent away to school makes a special tea for her, and allows her to choose which toys she shall take; and there is Mr Lloyd, the apothecary, who comes to see her when she becomes ill after being shut for hours (as punishment) in the room where her uncle died. 'I felt an inexpressible relief, a soothing conviction of protection and security, when I knew that there was a stranger in the room, an individual not belonging to Gatehead (the name of the house) and not related to Mrs Reed'. A negative recommendation perhaps, but he lifts her 'more tenderly than I had ever been carried or upheld before', and questions her gently and kindly. Very small bits of love, but better than none, and they keep the way open for the Superintendent of the frightful school to which she is sent. Miss Temple, though grave and not very intimate, does her best to mitigate the rigour and injustice of the system, defends Jane against false accusations passed on by her aunt, and boosts her confidence by assurances of trust. Anyone who as a child has suffered from a false accusation, and then being disbelieved, will recognize the comfort and gratitude of the child who says of a grown-up, as Jane says, 'I felt as I went on that Miss Temple fully believed me'. Later during her school career, as pupil and afterwards for two years as a teacher, 'her friendship and society had been my continual solace, she had stood me in stead of mother, governess, and latterly, companion. From the day she left I was no longer the same; with her was gone every settled feeling, every association that had made Lowood in some degree home to me. I had imbibed from her something of her nature and much of her habits; more harmonious thoughts, what seemed better regulated feelings had become the inmates of my mind . . . to the eyes of others, usually even to my own, I appeared a disciplined and subdued character'.

The relationship is more grave and restrained than spontaneous, but some of this lack is made good meanwhile by the saintly Helen Burns, who gives an unstinted friendship and support to the stormy, rebellious new pupil, so unlike herself. Helen's spiritual self-discipline is only equalled by her natural untidiness, and she is always in trouble but never resentful. Jane cannot understand this patient acceptance of ill-treatment, or fully approve it, but she develops a passionate love for Helen and tries to learn from her. Helen's friendship provides some of the intimacy, the physical tenderness and endearment, that Jane has lacked, but Helen dies of consumption, with Jane in her arms. There two 'mother substitutes' complement each other and produce the results mentioned.

A pleasanter, and considerably better observed, account of children's deprivation and its relief is in Jane Austen's *Mansfield Park*. Fanny is taken at the age of nine from her noisy, slatternly home, where her feckless mother had never had much value for this over-sensitive child, and her father's loud, and often boozy, geniality scared her horribly. Sir Thomas Bertram has decided to offer to bring up entirely one of the children of his wife's sister's needy family, and Fanny is the one he gets, since she is the least wanted. Hardly a propitious start in life, but Fanny's grand new home (but she is put to sleep in a fireless attic room near the servants) is even less satisfactory to a child needing love. At home she was at least useful and she belonged. At Mansfield Park she is an extra, taken out of charity, as her aunt Norris and her girl cousins are forever reminding her. Sir Thomas is so formal she is terrified of him, and his wife is good natured but too lazy to concern herself about anyone else and too stupid to notice if they need her concern. But Fanny, found crying on the stairs, is befriended by her big cousin Edmund, more out of a natural good-nature than from any special interest in the pale, tear-stained little 'extra'. But this is enough for Fanny. From that moment, Edmund is her god, which naturally affects him, too. 'Her countenance and a few artless words fully conveyed all their gratitude and delight, and her cousin began to find her an interesting object. He had never knowingly given her pain, but he now felt that she required more positive kindness ... From this day Fanny grew more comfortable ... The kindness of her cousin Edmund gave her better spirits with everybody else'.

The one passion of a timid, over-sensitive and deeply humble person is bound to be extremely vulnerable. Fanny suffers intensely when Edmund falls in love with vivacious Mary Crawford, though the idea that she herself has any claims on him has never occurred to her. His brief neglect of her, and his renewed care though he still dotes on Miss Crawford, throw her into a turmoil. Up to that time, 'she regarded her cousin as an example of everything good and great, as possessing worth which none but herself could ever appreciate, and as entitled to such gratitude from her as no feelings could be strong enough to pay. Her sentiments towards him were compounded of everything that was respectful, grateful, confiding and tender.' But by the time she is grown up this very love has given her a little confidence in herself as lovable. She knows she wants his love, hence her pain over his love for Mary. But still she cannot feel any right to his full devotion; 'to call it a loss, or a disappointment, would be a presumption ... to her, he could be nothing under any circumstances, nothing dearer than a friend. Why did such an idea occur to her even enough to be reprobated and forbidden? ... She had all the heroism of principle, and was determined to do her duty; but having also many of the feelings of youth and nature, let her not much be wondered at if . . . she seized the scrap of paper on which Edmund had begun writing to her, as a treasure beyond all her hopes'. Her love for Edmund is constant, and survives the persistent attentions of a more dashing suitor, even though she believes Edmund will certainly marry Mary Crawford. By that time she has given up pretending she doesn't want him herself, and Henry Crawford's unexpected and uncharacteristic devotion makes her realize she is not as insignificant as she thought. Even this equivocal love serves its purpose in helping Fanny to emotional maturity, and self-confidence without any arrogance. She visits her old home, and finds herself needed and appreciated by her younger sister: she can *give* love, as well as receive it, and she 'fills out' spiritually in this new experience. In the end Mary Crawford reveals her 'true nature', and the priggish Edmund walks out on her. Then, of course, he finally discovers that gentle Fanny is just what he was wanting all the time. Jane Austen is a little tart about this turn of events; I get the impression she had developed a dislike of the virtuous Edmund as the book progressed, and she evidently feels rather uncharitable towards her heroine for being so uncritically adoring. But it is all very satisfactory all the same. 'She was of course only too good for him; but as nobody minds having what is too good for them, he was very steadily earnest in pursuit of the blessing, and it was not possible that encouragement from her should be long wanting.' The happy ending is very proper but it is also likely. Here is the transition from dependent need on one side and generous support on the other to a mature mutuality. It is quite clear that, whatever he thinks, Edmund needs Fanny as much as she needs him. Since neither has the sort of 'block' that might require one or both to cling to the earlier roles, either as 'infant' or 'parent', they are able to progress to the new roles without a change of partners.

My third fictional example does not suffer from diffidence.

He has the tough, opportunistic outlook of the child who has had to fend for himself from babyhood. Kipling's *Kim* is the son of an Irish soldier and an English nurse-maid, who after his mother's death is reared by an opium-dazed bazaar-woman with whom his father lived until he died of opium. She feeds him, more or less, and makes sporadic attempts to keep him in European clothes, but is not really interested in him. The boy is clever, confident and friendly, the 'friend of all the world' but with no intimate relationships of any kind. He is the kind of boy who, if he continued in this way, would end up as a likeable and gifted criminal, ready to help people or to let them down with equal cheerfulness. Kim has one characteristic trait of the child with no close relationships, though kindly treated and even spoiled – he has no moral sense, even of the kind that operates in his own milieu. He does what he feels like and enjoys it, and acknowledges no obligations to anyone. But he meets the Lama, an old, wise, gentle and very holy Tibetan monk, who is on a pilgrimage to look for the 'River of the Arrow' which flowed where an arrow shot by the Lord Buddha hit the ground. None knows where it is, but to wash in it will bring full enlightenment. Kim sees the old man's complete ignorance of the ways of a strange country, and offers to beg his evening meal for him – mainly out of curiosity. But the Lama's trustfulness and directness – he treats the boy with respect, sweetness, and complete openness – gets through to Kim, who lives in a world where normally everyone is on the look-out to cheat everyone else and expects to be cheated themselves. He decides to go with the Lama on his search. His motive is still – at least consciously – curiosity and a desire to see new places, but the Lama's helplessness and dignity both influence him, and little by little he becomes attached to him, at first because the Lama needs his help, and the sense of being appreciated is good, but later – as he learns to know the Lama better –

because he senses in the old man a quality that is deeply attractive to him. Dedicated to total detachment from emotion though he is, the Lama in turn grows to love Kim, and this, with the Lama's own goodness and clarity of soul, binds the child to him. Kim is recognized as a white man's son, and is to be sent to school, and the Lama, struggling with his grief and the sense that he has sinned by loving the boy, offers to pay for him to have the best education possible. On the day Kim finally arrives at the school the Lama is waiting for him by the gate, and the boy leaps from the carriage that is taking him there to say goodbye. The Lama, his sensitive conscience struggling to reconcile his longing to see Kim with his pursuit of enlightenment and freedom from all human desires, has been reassured by tactful friends:

'I sent the money to suffice for one year, and then I came, as thou seest me, to watch for thee going up into the Gates of Learning. A day and a half have I waited – not because I was led by any affection towards thee – that is no part of the Way – but, as they said at the Tirthankars' Temple, because, money having been paid for learning, it was right that I should oversee the end of the matter. They resolved my doubts most clearly. I had a fear that, perhaps, I came because I wished to see thee – misguided by the Red Mist of affection. It is not so. . . .'

'But surely, Holy One, thou hast not forgotten the Road and all that befell on it. Surely it was a little to see me that thou didst come? . . . I am all alone in this land . . . I have no friend save thee, Holy One. Do not altogether go away'.

This is not the voice of the self-sufficient, unattached bazaar scamperer who was the 'Friend of all the World' for just as long as he chose and no longer. And his love is fully returned, for all the Lama's efforts at detachment.

'. . . Do not weep; for, look you, all Desire is an Illusion and a new binding upon the Wheel. Go up to the Gates of

Learning. Let me see thee go.... Dost thou love me? Then go, or my heart cracks.... I will come again. Surely I will come again'.

This is the outcome of a relationship that began because when Kim first saw the Lama he felt that 'this man was new in all his experience, and he meant to investigate further; precisely as he would have investigated a new building or a strange festival in Lahore city. The Lama was his trove, and he meant to take possession.' But instead he is possessed, by his growing love and need for the holy old man.

In time, when Kim leaves school and before he begins his career in the 'Great Game' – the secret service of India – he goes to serve the Lama as his disciple, and through hazardous wanderings, mixed with other adventures connected with the 'Game', he tends the old man untiringly. In the end he collapses from nervous over-strain, and part of his suffering before the final collapse is an hysterical fear that he has failed in devotion to his master, that he might have neglected him in any detail:

'I have walked thee too far; I have not considered the heat; I have talked to people on the road and left thee alone ... I have ... I have.... Hai ...! But I love thee ... and it is all too late ... I was child.... Oh, why was I not a man ...'.

Overborne by strain, fatigue and the weight beyond his years, Kim broke down and sobbed at the Lama's feet.

But he is no longer a child, he has become a man, and he owes it to the Lama. Kim, recovered from his illness, finds that the Lama, in a vision, has found his river and been cleansed and set free. At his death he is sure of enlightenment, and he will bring Kim to the same privilege. Kim is the same Kim – quick-witted, adventure-loving, opportunist and charming – but he is no longer a Peter Pan, he is a man capable of even passionate love, a whole, rounded, growing person. Kipling believed (as many with his kind of upbringing believed) that no woman could do this for a man, but only male love and friendship. He had the Greeks on his side. In an anti-woman culture, such a view is correct, for real love includes respect. But in any case what matters is the exchange of love.

All these examples are fictional. Others could be given, of brother and sister and similar relationships. These include both cases where the relationship is one of equality, and those in which one or other assumes a 'parental' role, at least for a time. And roles may vary and alternate.

I have not made use of autobiographies and case-histories here, because the novelist, as their creator, knows all about his characters, and his intuitive understanding makes them consistent. The observer of real people can only draw conclusions from what he is able to see, which may be incomplete in some vital respect. These well-known fictional examples make the point tellingly, but the examination of records of real lives bears out the more vivid verdict of fiction. Over and over again, obviously faulty relationships do not deform, or the personality emerges clear and mature in spite of deformity, whenever there has been real love at work. It can work at almost any stage of development, though the task is much more difficult in later life. The biographies of the famous provide evidence. To do it even faint justice would take up the whole of a book longer than this, but a handful of cases may help.

On the negative side Queen Elizabeth I is a good example of the child who is cared for, but without love. Primarily a stake in the game of power-politics, she learned to be as shrewd, wary, and opportunistic as Kim in his very different milieu, but for similar reasons. But no abiding love came into her life to alter the trend of her early development. She had ample opportunity to form 'free' relationships, and did so, on her own terms. The results of her inability to trust, or even to like anyone very much, modified the subsequent history of several countries. Possibly she developed a degree of reverence and trust for Cecil, but it looks rather more like the wary respect of one talented criminal for another even more gifted and ruthless.

Schopenhauer's mother was self-centred, vain and smug. Her son was sensitive, and admired her. She subdued him, belittled his achievements and frustrated his ambitions. He grew up to hate women (among other objects of hatred) and of course sex, with a virulent loathing; later he could conceive of love intellectually as the heroic self-giving that overcomes the egoism of 'will', but his own ability to love had never been cultivated, therefore there was nothing in him that could compass the heroism he acknowledged.

It is pleasanter to consider a couple of positive examples. Lady Jane Grey had a wretched childhood, badgered and punished and frightened by her ambitious and censorious parents. She had much less fun and more hardship than the little Princess Elizabeth, but love, in a very staid sober form, came to her in the person of her tutor, Roger Ascham. He was the only experience of personal concern and friendship in her chilly little life. She did not live long, but she seems to have shown a capacity for tender concern for others, and magnanimity in her unmerited persecutions, that she certainly did not learn from her parents.

Little is known with any certainty of the real life of the Israelite hero-king, David. He seems to have been a tough, shrewd soldier with a gift for leadership and an eye to the main chance, a superstitious but genuine piety, a capacity for ruthless selfishness, and an erratic notion of justice. In this picture it seems odd to discover the detail that, instead of triumphing over the death of his old enemy Saul, he composed a dirge for him, honoured his memory and (very characteristic, this) punished with death the man who helped Saul to his suicide on the battlefield, and told David the news in expectation of pleasing him. Saul's little lame grandson was sent for by David, now king in Saul's place, to 'eat at his table' forever. One can make a good guess at the reason for this uncharacteristic devotion and kindliness, for the love of David for Jonathan, Saul's son, is proverbial. In David's tough, dangerous existence Jonathan was a glimpse of another kind of life. Jonathan was generous and loving, and admired the vigour and courage of the guerilla-type leader. 'The soul of Jonathan was knit with the soul of David, and Jonathan loved him as his own soul'. But Jonathan's gentleness and dependence has its effect on David, if the tangled versions of the story can be relied on. Certainly this love of David and Jonathan endured as a firm ingredient in the stories, and it fits the facts. It has often been suggested that the relationship was homosexual, as if this somehow made it valueless. (If it was, it doesn't seem to have made David any less interested in women!) But, whatever the precise nature of the relationship, it was a loving one. David's love for Jonathan survived the young man's death in battle by his father's side, and permanently altered David's character, and even his rough-and-ready ethical standards.

Our final example is really an interlocking complex of examples, through three generations unusually well recorded by one of the characters concerned. The story begins with a girl very strictly brought up in a fairly well-to-do bourgeois household. The puritanical régime required the girls to be beaten and cowed into total submission, as the woman's role was that they should make a 'good marriage'. This particular girl was married young to a comfortably-off, good-natured, irreligious, bad-tempered, unfaithful man of middle age called Patricius, whose mother ran his household and intended to keep on doing so. He was fond of his wife in a way, and she avoided too many rows and beatings by giving in to him

over everything. Later, the couple became much closer, and
before he died he joined the Christian religion of his wife,
Monica. Maybe his motive was mainly to please her, but that
says a lot, and there seems to have been love in this marriage,
at that later stage. Meanwhile children were born. There
were three of them, probably, but only one is remembered
for his name was Augustine and it is to him we owe all there
is to know about the family. It was on this highly intelligent
boy that Monica concentrated her hopes, her ambitions, and
her frustrated affections. He was spoilt, and indulged, but
obliged to go to school because that was the road to success.
There he was beaten constantly, like every one else, learned
a great deal about sex, money, and how to get on in life,
and nothing whatever about love. His mother's fear of
alienating him and losing his affection led her to avoid making
any demands on him or trying to show him any good in life
beyond the satisfaction of his own desires. With her inbred fear
of and submission to the male this was natural enough. But
there was at least a little real love. Augustine knew how much
his mother centred on him and he seems to have tolerated
this and even responded to some extent, though he found her
Christian beliefs superstitious and feeble (in her version,
from her kind of family, they probably were) and her moral
exhortations ridiculous. When he left school he idled about
town for a year, until his parents could scrape enough money to
send him to university at Carthage. (How familiar it all is –
including his father's determination that his brilliant son shall
'get on', his chuckling pride in the boy's sexual exploits, and
Augustine's life-long contempt for his father who doted on
him.) At Carthage Augustine was the star of the university,
spoiled, praised, followed. In his arrogant way he experi-
mented sexually, intellectually, and emotionally. He did *feel*
things, he wasn't cold-hearted for all his selfishness. That much
his misguided parents had managed to develop in him. He

took a mistress – a usual thing – and fell in love with her, a less usual thing. She was of the slave class, and we know nothing of her except that Augustine loved her, apparently because *she* loved him so much that what was real in him responded. Anyway almost unbelievably, he was faithful to her for fifteen years. He took her home for a while, but there were such rows and scenes from his mother that he didn't stay long. He went back to Carthage, then took a job as a professor in Milan, and left secretly, to avoid more scenes. But he took his mistress with him, and they lived together in Milan and brought up their own child, a delicate and brilliant boy called Adeodatus, of whose intelligence Augustine was immensely proud. It has been plausibly suggested that the fact that Augustine and his mistress had only one son, and that one delicate, was due to their use of contraceptives, of which Augustine displayed an intimate knowledge, when he later condemned them. For he was at this time an adherent of the Manichean doctrines mentioned earlier, and therefore tried to avoid procreation. This may explain the equivocal nature of his intimate but curiously impersonal relationship with Adeodatus. It seems as if he couldn't quite accept that the boy was physically his son.

Ten years later, Monica joined him in Milan. Meanwhile her husband had died, and she had matured. She was less possessive and much more relaxed, but determined that Augustine should become (*a*) respectable and (*b*) a Christian, apparently in that order of importance. To Augustine it was the other way round, but the renunciation of sexual indulgence was to him a condition of the conversion he had begun to long for. He was too thoroughly Manichean in feeling, if no longer in doctrine, to distinguish sexual indulgence from sexual love, so finally – urged by Monica who had arranged a good marriage for him – he sent away his mistress. It was a terrible wound to him, but the quality of his mistress's love is shown by the fact that she not only went without bitterness but vowed herself to chastity thereafter, and also consented to leave her son with his father. You don't live with a woman like that for fifteen years without learning something about love, however reluctantly. Augustine did, and it showed later in his energetic service as a bishop, back in Africa, where he denounced the rich and served the poor, advised, helped, made peace, and became enormously beloved. But that was much later. Meanwhile, be became a Christian and also resolved on celibacy. Monica, released from the causes of her emotional outbursts, developed all the nicest aspects of her character, was devoted to her grandson, and she and Augustine became very close. She died soon afterwards, very content.

There was real love in Monica, in spite of all the distortions imposed on her by her upbringing and her marriage. She was wounded and she wounded her son, but neither of them was completely spoiled, and in both the capacity for love, which had never been completely crushed, finally came out on top. In some ways it is an appalling story of distorted emotions; from another point of view it shows how love can survive even such conditions.

Is it unimportant, then, whether the family structure is such as to deform human relations? If love comes through somehow, given the slightest chance, can we accept the distortions complacently? The conclusion to be drawn is almost the opposite. If love is so powerful a force that it can survive and triumph over almost any obstacles, then what could it do if it were given full rein in human hope, not accidentally but deliberately, with full understanding?

V

LOVE AND COMMUNITIES

THE evidence so far accumulated shows that the organization of human life, both public and private, tends to the suppression, direction, or canalization of the power we call 'love'. It does this because love is the great breaker of barriers and upsetter of habits and traditions, and barriers, habits and traditions are the things that make it possible for people to get on with their lives, in the particular conditions in which they live. They restrain and re-train and explain the power that, unorganized, seems so dangerous and frightening because it exposes depths in human beings that cannot be accommodated in any given social order. It reveals desires and hopes that cannot be satisfied.

Yet love is also the healer, the reconciler, the inspirer, the creator of community and the bond of social relationships.

This may seem contradictory, but it is only apparently so. Love seems 'dangerous' because it breaks down barriers raised by society for its own purposes, such as those of class, race, or sex; but the breaking of unwanted barriers reconciles enemies, cements loyalties, unites people in the service of their family, or tribe, drives them to achievements they would not otherwise manage except under the stress of extreme fear. It is the power of love to create communion by breaking through to new and recognizably important areas of personality that make it both fearful and desirable. And, as we have seen, whether it is desired or not, encouraged or not, it happens. But, as I suggested in the last chapter, the social structure is by no means irrelevant to the result in terms of love. Whether love can develop its full potential, or whether it is obliged to be secretive, disruptive and to a great extent ineffective depends on the type of society in which it occurs. What is more, societies such as ours that pay lip-service at least to the value of loving personal relationships can also use this very fact to distract attention – and love – from the need for or even the possibility of love in the wider political sphere. So we can have happy loving families who are indifferent to the horrors suffered by the homeless, and content that the normal treatment for a seriously disturbed 'delinquent' is a stiff term in Borstal. This is the especial sin of the 'bourgeois' society though it is only one form of the perennial attempt to render love 'harmless' and restrict its operations. Those, in fact, who attack the 'bourgeois' family ideal on the grounds that it deforms the individual's capacity for relationships are attacking it on its strongest side. More cogent is the charge that it confines love to the 'private' domain and so, in effect, to a privileged class of people who are not threatened by homelessness, hunger, imprisonment or enslavement, at home or abroad.

The conclusion is drawn, correctly, that the social structure must be so altered that *all* human beings are in a position to achieve the 'good life' and secure personal relationships. The corollary to this has always seemed to be, however, that a just, free, loving *society* must necessarily be opposed to the idea of unique and close personal relationship, and in particular to close family ties. Thomas More's *Utopia* is not, as many people believe, his idea of the 'perfect' society. It is his attempt to show that even by the aid of natural reason alone men could create a just, free and contented society. In that case, he implied, how much worse is the failure of so-called Christians, with all the advantages of Christ's revelation to help them, to create a society even passably just. But even the modified perfection of his Utopians is based on the dilution of family ties (by means of communal eating and education of children apart from their parents), in favour of civic loyalty and service. More, like the Israelis and many left-wing societies or would-be societies, assumed an opposition between close personal ties and love of the community at large. Plato did it even more thoroughly, and his *Republic* proposed strict genetic planning, and the use of the selected couples purely for breeding purposes, the children's education being taken over entirely by the State. This is, or was, the ideal of most present-day socialists. Marx himself, however, distinguished between the *abuse* of family ties and their existence, which he did not regard as in themselves enemies to socialism. Large-scale industry he says, 'in overturning the economic foundation on which the traditional family and family labour corresponding to it was based, had also dissolved all traditional family ties. . . . It was not, however, the misuse of parental authority that created the capitalistic exploitation, whether direct or indirect, of children's labour, but on the contrary it was the capitalistic mode of exploitation which, by sweeping away the economic basis of parental authority, made its exercise degenerate into a misuse of power.' He goes on to suggest that the increased importance of the roles of women and young people in industry may provide a basis for a 'higher form of the family', and what he means by a 'higher form' turns out to be something similar to the 'extended family' of some primitive cultures, but without the restriction of elaborately coded blood-relationships.

The various attempts to produce a practicable version of Marxist teaching, as well as similar ideal societies in fact and in imagination, have all depended on careful and doctrinally 'correct' instruction, of the young especially. It is not only Christians who have assumed that if you tell a child often enough and simply enough that God – or socialism – requires that he love his comrade he will do so. If he does do so this is assumed to be the result of the teaching. If he does not it is because he did not learn properly, or was misled by false teaching.

Recent studies of group behaviour, however, seem to cast some doubt on this. Although what people are taught about their obligations towards each other is obviously important in determining who, and when, they love, the actual occurrence of love as a force, both cohesive and goal-orientated, depends on other factors. If effective teaching on the importance of compassion and brotherly concern were sufficient to bring it into existence the continuous, imaginative advertising campaign on behalf of famine and war relief organizations would have resulted in the virtual overturning of the world economic system, in favour of the 'developing' countries. In fact, no such outbreak of love has occurred or is likely to occur, otherwise such advertising would probably be forbidden by law, since the economic stability of the Western world depends on the non-development of the 'developing' countries. A serious outbreak of love in the world would bring the markets crashing down. This may sound shockingly cynical, but an examination of the figures for world trade confirms it.

A thorough account of the research and the evidence is impossible here, but a few accounts of group-reactions may help to widen the concept of love, which has up to now been examined mainly at the inter-personal level, with the social organization often in the role of villain.

In order to give an idea of a relation between community and individual which we might reasonably describe as loving, I quote from the work of a Marxist[1] who is also a Christian, and who states the ideal in terms of real political relationships. He describes first the capitalist society in which there is 'tension

[1] TERENCE EAGLETON, *The New Left Church*, p. 165. Sheed & Ward 1966.

between the way (a person) is used within another's project, as an object, and his own sense of personal value, as a subject'. This tendency to make people into objects is, as we have seen, the one great enemy of love. Whether the 'objectifying' is done for the sake of sexual pleasure, or moral domination, or the ambitions of the state, or the survival of the social organism, the effect is the same. And the 'cure' proposed is terribly simple:

> The way this condition can be resolved, theoretically, is by the elimination of the conditions in which men can be objects, tools, to each other. What is needed is a society in which all men can be equally and simultaneously *subjects*, ordering their lives with the kind of free autonomy which at present, in capitalism, is available only to a minority.
>
> The radical response to an alienated society is the response of *community* ... to affirm that men can be free only in genuine equal relationship, not by avoiding relationships (as with some kinds of individualist anarchism), or by enslaving others in order to ensure one's own precarious freedom (as with capitalism).... We need to build a political society where the unity of the whole community can be interiorized within each member of it, where individual subjects are both reconciled in face to face relationships, between themselves, and, in and through this, reconciled in a whole community. This last point is very important: the reconciliation of two persons, in direct relationship, must share in and be re-constituted by the whole reconciliation of men in the complete community. ... A face to face relationship, simply by being most intensely itself, must point beyond itself to the wider community from which it springs, and which is its ground.

Unfortunately, as we have seen, loving relationships normally find themselves in opposition to the wider community, or at best given a sort of liberal political vacuum in which to work off their dangerous energy without wider repercussions.

There has never yet been a large political entity that corresponds to the description just given, but if it is to make sense at all it must be at least a human possibility. Does this happen at all?

It happens in a way that verifies the description very accurately, if 'the wider community from which it springs' is understood to mean not necessarily the social system within which the face-to-face relationships happen to be placed, but rather the one from which it gets its inspiration and 'drive'. The community that Terence Eagleton was thinking of in the above passage is one whose model is the Christian liturgical assembly in which the focus of love is Christ, and it is in him that individuals are reconciled and committed to love in their face-to-face relationships. Christ constitutes the nature of the community at large, hence there is no opposition but a necessary correlation between group adherence and face-to-face relationship. The same can be seen in families where the quality of the parents' love creates the community as a whole, and within it and by it the other face-to-face relationships are possible and meaningful. Another example of this is the Jewish community described in the first chapter, in which close family relationships are validated and sustained by the wider community of faith, so that they 'point beyond' themselves.

More detailed evidence of how this happens, and when and why it doesn't happen, is to be found in recent sociological studies of communities of manageable size. An especially interesting study (all the more convincing because of its limited aim and moderate style) is *Small Social Groups in England*, by Margaret Phillips, subtitled 'a real life study', which is exactly what it is.

The examples chosen were all studied under war-time conditions, a circumstance which destroyed some of the normal security of the people concerned and freed them to form new associations. The largest community studied is a village, most of them are smaller. They include 'accidental' groups such as a group of men in an internment camp, 'semi-accidental' groups like the loose organization for evacuated mothers in a seaside resort, and 'deliberate' groups like a religious community. The interesting thing is that whether the people are thrown together by circumstances or freely choose to join a group the same 'rules' seem to operate in the creation or disruption of relationships.

The community of evacuated mothers need not have happened at all. Unlike the cases of people obliged to associate and free only as to whether they will do so in a positive or negative way, these women could have spent the period of their residence in the town in isolation from one another, or perhaps associated in chance individual friendships. Some could have been assimilated individually into the host community, and this did happen in a few cases, while others preferred to hold aloof and refused to make friends. The association of these women came about through the initiative of two sisters already living there who were looking for something useful to do, and found this idea 'an answer to prayer'. It is actually quite normal for a community to come into being because someone is 'looking for work' and recognizes something that needs doing. This type of leadership provides a natural focus for the life of the community from the beginning. These two created a 'home' for the evacuated women and their children, who had been uprooted and were lonely, friendless, and often worried about their husbands and the homes they had left. As one of them put it 'I found myself again'. It was not all plain-sailing. The mothers came from different areas and different backgrounds, their insecurity made them touchy and there were rows. The two 'wardens' found the solution was to give them something to do together. They gave parties for the children, the mothers all helping. They organized 'spring-cleaning' days, arranged fêtes to help local charities. The women got to know each other as they did things together, and good will and even affection sprang up. They began to do things for each other, visited those in hospital, helped with the children. Because evacuated families came and left irregularly it was not possible in this case for the mothers to have a permanent committee to run the Centre themselves, but they were expected to make suggestions and carry them out. Their ideas led to the setting up of a communal laundry, baths, nursery, cook-house for making jam and so on, to vary their diet. But the two women who were in charge provided a focus for the whole scheme. They were there to be referred to, to settle quarrels, and above all to represent the fact of the Centre and the kind of thing it was. If they had withdrawn the disruptive forces that are always present in a group would have got out of hand and the scheme would have collapsed.

In this group the needs of the people concerned created the association and gave it its character. It had no other purpose but to satisfy them. A team working a threshing-machine is an example of a group which is created and determined by the demands of a process, regardless of their own wishes. An account given by a member of the team shows that human association is almost nil while on the job. Initiative and inter-relation is only possible if something goes wrong, or if work halts for a whole and allows time and 'psychological space' for people to be aware of each other. The normal attitude of people to each other in such a situation is indifference, or hostility if someone seems to have an easier job, or does it badly and therefore needs to be helped. This can be seen on a much larger scale in the whole field of industrial relations.

A group created for a purpose beyond itself need not be so completely subordinated to the demands of the purpose if it is one which engages their enthusiasm. But even enthusiasm does not always counteract the de-humanizing effect of

K

subordination to a purpose. The 'wider community' within which relationships occur, if they are allowed to occur at all, must be one that envisages and actively desires such relationships. In this book three Christian communities are studied, one a Catholic convent of a strict and old-fashioned but fervent type, another an evangelical community including married people with families, but living a common life, and the third a Quaker 'Meeting'. All three groups were founded in order to follow Christ as fully as possible. In the convent friendship between individuals is discouraged in favour of a more general devotion, and in the Protestant community, though family life is encouraged, the personal relationships of individuals are subordinated to the service of the whole group. Those who 'withdraw' into close personal relationships are told that they are depriving the rest. All letters are left unsealed. Most meals are in common, and much else also.

The Friends' Meeting is not a 'whole-life' association, but in the Meeting itself there is great emphasis on discovering a common mind. Members who contributed to this study noticed that the activities which grew out of the Meeting and were organized by members were important to the sense of love in community. Where these failed recrimination and division often became apparent. In all these cases the harmony and charity of the group depend usually on the work of a few people who are not necessarily in direct control in a governing sense but who are a 'focus' of spiritual energy. In the convent the Superior is the one who sets the tone for the whole community, for she 'represents Christ' quite explicitly. The Protestant community gets its character from its founder, a theologian, and his principles are worked out and applied by discussion and agreement between the full adult members of the community. The success and harmony of the Friends' Meeting often, in practice, depends on the tact and helpfulness of one person, the Clerk, but the overall desire of the group to be in love and harmony makes this much more likely to succeed than in the case of the evacuated mothers. Among the Friends, the practice of silence is a help to this end, allowing each person the opportunity to recollect the purpose of membership, set aside 'disruptive' feelings and desires, and turn to God, who is the 'centre' of all three groups. Silence is also emphasized in the other two communities, but the purpose there is at least partly negative also: to make fewer opportunities for mutual irritation or the random expression of ill-feeling. But it is clear that however important the influence of the person or small group at the heart of the larger group may be, it is not enough to keep them together, and make 'reconciliation' possible, unless there is also the sense of a wider commitment, some aim or cause that gives meaning to the association. This cause can be strong enough to keep people devoted to it even when human love and leadership are apparently absent.

In a hospital group studied, the disruption of the work by personal antagonism is always a danger, and is controlled by the rigid conventions of discipline which make casual contact between different grades of staff virtually impossible during working hours. This quasi-religious hierarchy is so wholeheartedly enforced that even in off-duty periods normal contact is unlikely. Discipline is arbitrary and often harsh, though personal kindliness mitigates its severity in practice. This is a good example of how devotion to the work itself creates a sense of 'belonging' and even a sort of interior reconciliation even when the organization apparently suppresses every expression of community. The same used to be true of many convents. A nurse quoted in this study remarked that it was only in the early days of her training that she got a real sense of support and warmth, from the Sister in charge of probationers. Later she felt isolated, and any human satisfaction could only be found in brief relationships with patients, and in the satisfaction of helping them. She remembered also brief and important moments when human feeling 'broke through', as when a doctor came, during the night, to see a boy on whom he had operated. His joy and relief on realizing that the risky operation had succeeded were communicated to the nurse as she met his eyes. But that was all. Hospital etiquette made any more extensive 'sharing' of the burdens and achievements of the common work out of the question.

In a school the hierarchy is generally less evident, and depends more on seniority, relation to the Head, prestige of the subject taught, or sheer personality. The whole situation is more flexible and therefore has greater potential both for creative private and group relationship, and also for factions, and rivalries, persecutions and so on. Again, the overall character of the staff as a group (and therefore of the whole school) will depend to a great extent on the Head, who may also be the founder, i.e. creator of the whole ethos and sense of direction of the community, even if he or she is not the first Head. A determined and strong personality among the staff can disrupt the group, but on the whole a staff that has imaginative, sympathetic leadership from the Head will be a good setting for the development of individual friendship and co-operation. He or she provides the definition of the 'wider community' in which the face-to-face relationships find their meaning and energy.

An unusual type of community was created by a New York Evangelical pastor who drew together a group of young gangsters, drug-addicts and so on, of both sexes, from the Bowery slums. He eventually bought a home for them. The association was quite free, they came because they had been 'converted' or wanted to be. Only their own will to win through, and the love of the pastor and his wife and helpers, brought or kept them there. But, being there, they were not only helped individually, they helped each other. Often a boy or girl would be pulled through a 'bad patch' (and the 'patches' of a drug-addict 'drying out' are very bad indeed) by another who had had the same experience. There was real joy and love in the house, and it was made explicit, and strengthened, and friction lessened, by prayer – loud, vocal, continued spontaneous prayer. The pastor and his wife kept the place together, but the 'wider community' was not wholly 'theirs'. As in other cases where an association is formed for a purpose beyond itself, the 'founder' is in some sense also a symbol of what the community is for. This one was for the regeneration of these young people, but this was felt to be possible only because of Christ. The 'beyond' of the community was 'Christ', but in him each one found personal reconciliation and love meaningful and possible.

Another example of the same type of group creation is provided by the extraordinary organization of the 'Compagnons d'Emmaus', now a world-wide organization. It began with the haphazard arrival of a few down and outs, ex-criminals, tramps, etc., at a huge ruined old house owned by a French priest, Abbé Pierre. They were all kinds including some militant atheists. They just turned up, looking for shelter, because they had nowhere else to go. But homeless families also turned up, by chance at first, and then because the word went round. Soon the Abbé was forced to realize the problem of homelessness. He, like others, had thought it was just a matter of a few tramps, but discovered that hundreds of working families were homeless, and the government would do nothing. It is a story worth reading (in two books *Abbé Pierre and the Rag-Pickers* and *Ragman's City*), but the interesting point for the study of community is that the Abbé decided to *use* the chance group of down and outs to help these families. He organized them to collect saleable refuse from dumps and dustbins, and in house-to-house collections of 'rubbish' from attics. The sale of all this brought in a little money, they used it to put up small houses on a bit of waste-land, defying the bye-laws. One little but decent house after another went up, the men recalled disused skills in plumbing and so on. It was a drop in the ocean, but it got things moving. The opposition aroused, and the press comment, in the end forced government action on housing and the movement spread. But meanwhile the 'socially inadequate' outcasts who had dossed down at the old house had become a tough team of reliable, hard-working, self-respecting people, intent on carrying out an important job of work. There were bad moments, failures and betrayals, but it worked. The Abbé was the one who kept the thing going, but it didn't go because of him, nor for the sake of the men themselves. They were reconciled, and learned to love, because they 'found them-selves' in the setting of a 'wider community' whose purpose was the salvation of families from degradation and despair.

Consideration of these few examples shows that there are two basic conditions without which love will not occur in a group, of whatever size. First of all there has to be what might be called a 'focus' of the community. This may be a cause, or project on which the members are engaged, or it may be a personality to whom the others are devoted. It may be temporary, like the building of a recreation centre, or long-term, like the maintenance of a village community, or a hospital or a religion. The focus may be 'symbolic' in the sense that what is being worked at immediately is only part of the service of some wider concept such as 'freedom' or 'God' or 'socialism', and in this case the wider concept is normally embodied in some person, who may be a practical leader but may be purely symbolic, like a constitutional monarch. When the 'focus' in this wider sense is not vivid to the members the creation of love in the group will depend on the actual human leaders to a much greater extent. *They* must have a very clear idea of what they are trying to do, as in the case of the group of evacuated mothers. Here the two founders knew what they were about, the mothers often did not, and short-term common projects were used as a cohesive influence in place of any common idea or intention. The same sort of attitude can be seen in the much larger units of Churches or organizations with a strong hierarchical and centralized mentality. The 'ordinary' members are not expected to understand very clearly what it is all about, those in authority will do the thinking and planning, all the others have to do is obey. This has been the attitude of the Catholic Church to its laity, of most hospitals to the junior nurses and even more to the patients, of old-fashioned schools to the pupils, of factory managements to the workers, and so on. This principle of 'paternalism' *may* be the only possible way to cope with a particular case. It was with the evacuated mothers, whose brief stay and insecure state of mind made it important above all to give them support, rather than to demand initiative and decisions. But when it is *not* necessary 'paternalism' has a disruptive rather than a cohesive effect on a community, as in a school with an authoritarian Head, in which the staff are often discontented, jealous and irritable and the children either hostile or bored and passive. Reconciliation and the outbreak of love are unlikely in such an atmosphere.

The 'focus' of a community, therefore, can be all kinds of things but it does, at some point, articulate itself through a leader or leaders, either chosen or simply arising by force of personality. The success of this person in creating the conditions for love will depend on his or her willingness to subordinate personal ambition and satisfaction both to the needs of the individuals in the group *and* to the overall aim of the group. Even when the latter is summed up in the former, it cannot be achieved if the members can see their own satisfaction as its only purpose. Among some at least, some of the time, the leader must evoke a generous, outward-turning attitude. Even when a group exists purely in order to benefit its members, if love is to occur at all this 'benefit' must assume a sort of collective personality. Thus members of a 'gang', formed purely for fun and adventure, will spontaneously develop (given good leadership) a form of group solidarity, and will protect, help and comfort each other in trouble.

The second basic condition actually grows out of the first. The need for a 'focus' demands also that the group should 'do something' about whatever their aim or *raison d'être* may be. This is obvious when a group is formed for a specific purpose, but it is equally true when the group is an accidental one, with no special reason except that they happen to be there. A group of this kind, such as people who happen to turn up at the pub on a Sunday about the same time, may continue simply to be present, and reasonably friendly and chatty, and no more. This kind of non-loving though quite amicable grouping occurs among people who are on the same bus every day or work in the same office or factory where the job does not require any but mechanical co-operation. This type of association only changes in character and becomes a community if it discovers some common aim. This aim may be simply to *be* a community, rather than just a crowd. In an office this may lead to giving a party, so that people can 'get to know each other', or to the calling of meetings to discuss the work of the firm and make suggestions for action. A pub group may decide to organize an old-people's outing. A village may develop a strong coherence over-night in response to a threat such as the flooding of the village for a new reservoir. A similar, more constructive, coherence can occur when a village or small town undertakes some major initiative, like the one in Holland that decided to look after the mentally ill in their homes instead of in hospital. In all these cases, a group of people who formerly just happened to be together is brought into existence as a real community by *doing* something together, which they *want* to do. *Forced* common action (like the threshing team) does not do so, though a common dislike of it, and opposition to it, may be cohesive.

There is no obvious limit to the size of the community which can achieve this situation, in which reconciliation and love can occur in face-to-face relationships, *in* and *because* of the nature of the wider community. It is easiest to observe this in small groups, but it can happen in very big ones. During the 'blitz', the whole of London developed a sense of community so strong it was almost palpable. Everyone was a friend, anyone would help anyone else even if they had never met before – even sometimes if they had been life-long enemies. It was not merely hatred of the Nazis, or fear, that brought people together. It was simply the common struggle to survive, to be human and go on living, that created that extraordinary but temporary solidarity.

The same sudden comradeship occurred during the early days of the Russian revolution, and in other revolutions. It seems to be operating fairly widely, though not universally, in Cuba, and to a lesser extent, though very intensely where it does occur, in China. Where people are inspired either by a threat, or by good leadership, or commonly both, to take on a great common effort, the result is a community in which reconciliation is possible between individuals, not in opposition to or in detachment from the overall political organization, but because of it.

The fact that in so many cases such an experience of true community has been limited, either in numbers or in time or both, is due to the failure of one or other of the two conditions.

The 'focus' can fail, perhaps because the leadership ceases to be convincing or sensible, or because the proposed purpose has been achieved and nothing else seems sufficiently important. The overall aim may lose its appeal, because people are more comfortable and don't feel the need to struggle any more. A general increase in the level of comfort and safety is the most common cause of the loss of community, because the hope of achievement is replaced by fear of losing what has been gained. In the absence of the sort of leadership that might convince people of the importance of goals other than their own security, this kind of normal selfishness is the complete preventative of community. All societies have to cope with this problem, for if the sense of community is completely lost it becomes extremely difficult to maintain a viable political organism at all. All societies have to be able to rely on at least minimal co-operation in common tasks, such as the protection of life and property and the creation of means of distribution and exchange. Generally, a society also wants to assure the education of its children, the defence of its territory, and probably the means of transport. That means money, which means taxes, and a certain minimum of civic responsibility has to be assumed. The tax system, the law-enforcement system, and the educational system, would all collapse if everyone told lies to everyone else all the time and took what he wanted when he wanted it. However high the crime rate, the assumption is that only a minority are criminals, or the system is unworkable. If this assumption is proved mistaken, or if the governing power is itself criminal, the only alternative is to rule the country by means of fear, enforcing the will of the minority on the rest by sheer terror. It never works for very long, anyway. Therefore, governments spend a lot of effort trying to create a sense of purpose, and a confidence in leadership, among the people at large. Patriotism, nationalism, and so on, are ways of describing the type of emotion which is evoked in order to create a sense of community among people who have nothing much in common except the fact that they live within the same geographical area. When it works it does indeed create a real, if limited, kind of community, but it works only when there is in fact something to be done – a war to be fought, cities to be rebuilt, new lands to be opened up and developed, or conquered. Once the work is over, when the point of the association is once more merely mutual advantage, then the sense of community fades. But the organization of such a society can continue to work if the sense of community can be somehow transferred to a symbolic or religious sphere, where the common activity really is activity, and does seem to 'point beyond' the individual, by means of religious activity and leadership. The practical aim may well be, as in tribes whose way of life is agricultural or pastoral, purely the benefit of each one, but this benefit is conceived in religious terms, applying to the whole community and making of it a 'person' who may be validated by relation to a god, or the ancestors who 'created' the people, or simply to the sense of 'Divinity'. This is the nearest English word for the complicated concept by which the Dinka people (studied by Lienhardt) describe their sense of the omni-presence of the transcendent principle which informs their understanding of life in all its manifestations, both at the level of particular people, animals, and things, and at the level of wider but practical concepts such as 'life', 'sky', 'fertility' and so on.

As Lienhardt says in his *Social Anthropology*, a religion provides a distinctive patterning of experience, a map of the psyche and the world which, for believers, is held to represent the situation of man in true proportion and scale. And in this 'patterning' the cohesive element, that which both expresses and creates the experience of community, is generally what we call 'sacrifice'. This does not necessarily mean blood sacrifices, or anything painful or difficult to do. The painfulness is incidental just as the love of two people for each other may entail suffering, but it is not the suffering that matters, it is the love which is so important that even acute suffering can be endured for its sake. A leader of an African church, Isaiah

Shembe, is quoted by Lienhardt as saying 'sacrifices hold people together by blood. The Gate of Heaven is opened through sacrifices'. And he goes on 'the suggestion that sacrifice "holds people together" does not derive exclusively from Christianity – it is possible to see considerable sociological truth in Shembe's view. . . .' Common sacrifice is a sign of common interests and asserts and promotes them. It represents a common life, and not only on the ideal or metaphorical plane, but in the day-to-day practical human co-operation. In our society the myth and rituals of national history and custom still help to preserve some sense of community, though less and less effectively.

This religious aspect of the creation of community is much better appreciated now than when many Europeans thought of a religion as concerned with the individual relation to 'the beyond', while the social arrangements of everyday life were independently created and could get on quite well on their own. But religion is the articulation of a people's self-knowledge, it is the 'language' of their awareness of life and love. If it is destroyed by contact with stronger and incompatible cultures the confidence and purpose which bound people together fails also. They disintegrate socially, as individuals they become depressed, their fertility declines, and they may die out altogether, since their lives have no longer any meaning. This shows, in a negative sense, the close connection between the community bond and the health of individual face-to-face relationships. The total destruction of the sense of community makes individual relationships virtually impossible also. The lack of love in the community follows the loss of purpose, leadership and 'focus'. The loss of confidence in the community destroys self-confidence and therefore the ability to 'go out' in the openness of love between individuals. This loss is best described as a loss of religion, even when the set of concepts referred to is of a secular kind.

Our own society has not totally lost the sense of community, there is at least some sense of 'belonging' to something or other even when the overall political structure has little to do with it and may even work against it. In our kind of society the two conditions for love in the political context seldom occur in the wider national field, where 'politics' means diplomatic manoeuvring for advantage, and 'leadership' means the skill to do this more cleverly. No real 'focus' of community is possible in such a set-up, and no common work emerges. But in the love-vacuum created by this kind of generalized selfishness sub-societies take over the real human political reality. In them community can still occur, when people are drawn together by the focus (and associated tasks) of groupings according to class, profession, religion, race, intellect, political ideology – even locality in some cases, such as a town threatened by a motor-way, an airport, a 'new town' or 'blacks'.

From this last example it will be clear that such close and enthusiastic communities are not always *loving*. Hate can be extremely cohesive, and works faster and more completely than love. This is why revolutionary leaders tend to rely on hate to rouse people to action. This fact may be allied to the one I noticed in the first chapter, that the energy we would in some circumstances describe as 'love' may emerge in other forms when it is prevented from taking those of love.

From all that has been said up to now, it seems that a 'wider community' truly capable of being the cause and setting of good face-to-face relationships can only happen on a small scale with any deliberation, and that otherwise it only happens when emergency, or some huge upheaval, draw people together in a virtually inescapable task, or when political leaders deliberately evoke the necessary emotional power by the creation of a sense of the urgency of some task.

But even so it must be at least theoretically possible to draw people into a wider community of a truly reconciling kind by proposing to them purposes which are creative and saving on a national and even international scale. If this does not happen it is not because human beings are too naturally depraved to appreciate such purposes; the experience of small groups proves that this is not so. The reason in the case of the West is that the weight of our culture comes down heavily on the side of self-improvement, independence, making good, getting on, getting ahead and all the rest of it. Basically and constantly, we instil into children the notion that they are against others, and others against them. If they fail they go under. The way to survive is to stay on top and not look down. Our culture, all our economic system, our conditions of employment, our fundamental value-judgements of people – in fact the whole of our language of human association, down to and including sexual relations and progress at school – are based on the idea of rivalry, each against the other. In such an atmosphere it is hardly surprising that the effect of any attempt to create community on the basis of response to people who are hungry, homeless, frightened or in pain is minimal.

This state of affairs can only be changed if people are brought up differently. In the small, family situations it was clear that the ability to love generously was greatly dependent on secure and loving relationships with parents or parent substitutes. But if this is ever to reach beyond the sphere of strictly inter-personal relationships it is necessary for the child and adolescent to have experience of the possibility of such a wider reference of love. The very emotional tone we give to the word 'politics' shows how little we expect it to have anything to do with love. The same applies to words like 'organization', 'society' and 'authority'. These, which normally relate to numerically large associations of human beings, are thought of as naturally opposed to love, which is seen as essentially a private matter, confined to non-working hours, in our own private home.

If this re-orientation of thinking and feeling about the political dimension of human life is to come about it will have to begin in the schools. Unfortunately, most schools operate according to the assumptions just mentioned about the essential privacy of love, and this is so even when the personal relations between staff and children are good. Competition and rivalry are basic to the work system, and authority is *assumed* to consist in the assertion and exercise of arbitrary power. Any consultation, consensus, or preceding discussion is regarded as a dilution of authority, *even when this is held to be desirable*. Yet it is apparent in the examples of groups quoted above that authority in the form of effective leadership is one of the factors in creating that essential 'focus' of community-self-awareness which makes love in the political dimension possible at all.

In order to demonstrate the feasibility of a political community which loves, and creates love, I shall present in some detail one magnificent real-life example of the creation of community in the most inauspicious conditions. But since the whole meaning and success of this experiment turned on the nature of leadership, I want first to lay the ghost of 'authority' as the inevitable killer of love, the destroyer of initiative, the flattener of individual effort and ideas. This is done very amusingly in relation to that (up to now) most authoritarian of all organizations, the Roman Catholic Church, in an article in an American magazine, in which Andrew Greeley freely imagines the election of a young American as Pope, and supposes that he would immediately call a Press conference. The new Pope refuses to be addressed as 'Holy Father' since he is 'not holy, and not anybody's Father', and is dressed in a grey suit and paisley tie. He announces that he intends to consult the other bishops thoroughly about all controversial questions before giving an opinion, he also intends to get the opinion of experts in the relevant fields, to set up as soon as possible an international network of senates to collect, collate and present public opinion and need to Rome, separate the legislative and judicial functions of the Church, bring canon law up to date and make it 'live', publish the financial situation of the Vatican ('as soon as I can figure out what it is'), have bishops elected as in the early Church, and abolish heresy trials, censorship, and other outdated customs.

After all this, the reporter for the *Washington Post* sums up what is likely to be the general reaction of people whose notion of authority is the one I outlined above – that is, 'authoritarian', arbitrary, and oppressive. I quote his question and the answer of the imaginary new Pope, because it makes the point excellently about the nature of leadership in a community that takes love seriously:

Q. From all you've said so far, Sir, it would seem that you are really anticipating *a very notable decline in Papal authority*. (My italics). I wonder if you could tell us whether you think this is a drastic change in Church doctrine?

A. Well, I don't know where you got that idea; I must say, as a matter of fact, I think what I'm talking about is a rather notable increase in Papal authority. A Pope who is informed by his colleagues in the Synod and by the lay people of the world and a network of lay associations, who has for his advisers the best theologians and scholars in the world, who makes informed decisions and can rely on co-operation with these decisions, isn't exactly a weak leader. On the contrary, I think he's a pretty strong one. It is not my intention to weaken the powers of the Papacy at all, but to strengthen the powers of the Papacy and the reforms that I've discussed are designed to do just that. I might also say that it's probably going to increase the work of the Papacy. . . . You know it's kind of easy to make unilateral decisions, but it's awfully hard to gain consensus. . . . It seems to me that the most important job of a man in my position is not to answer questions, but to ask them; *not to supply people with answers, but to challenge them to find out what the answers are.*

This imaginary Press Conference is a bit of fun, but it makes the point all the more effectively. The point is, from the point of view of the study of love, that leadership is an essential part of the creation of a political situation in which love can and probably will occur. But the kind of leadership is crucial. Any discussion about love that is realistic ends up discussing authority, which is (or should be) another word for leadership. But leadership, or authority, can be and are so often abused that (like those dangerous 'family relationships') the temptation is to condemn the thing itself and try to do without. The result is not something better but the emergence of undercover leadership of a kind which is much more likely to be destructive precisely because its nature is disguised. Anyone who doubts this had better read *Animal Farm*. 'All animals are equal, but some are more equal than others', and they get their way without the 'others' realizing what's happening.

It is important, therefore, if love is to be regarded as a possibility not only in private but in public to recognize squarely the place that leadership occupies in creating the conditions for love, or for suppressing it. Then we shall be in a position to judge the qualities of actual leadership by realistic and human standards, and be able roundly to condemn the wrong kind while encouraging the right kind.

The example I have chosen has created something of a stir. The full study, available in paperback[1], is essential reading. The name of the book is the name of a school, *Risinghill*, and the subtitle, *Death of a Comprehensive School*, indicates that the book has a tragic ending. It has, but possibly this death

[1] LEILA BERG: *Risinghill, Death of a Comprehensive School*, Pelican 1968.

will lead to a resurrection of hope in the lives of many children, for their teachers and parents might never have heard that it is possible to educate people to love, by loving them, if this school had not been killed by hate, prejudice and fear, and if this outrage had not roused public opinion, and driven someone to write a book documenting the full extent of the achievement, and of the tactics that secured its closure.

Risinghill School was built in one of the worst districts of London, an area notorious for its appalling housing conditions and the resulting vice and gangsterism. When families live in one or two damp, rat-infested rooms the children play in the street, and the police distrust them on principle. The mother may go out to work, so the children can't get in unless they climb through the window. And if the mother's 'work' includes bringing men home the child may be excluded for this reason also. Like the slums of all big cities, it is an area where sex is normally a matter of exploitation, furtive experiment or brutal adventure; where marriage tends to be a long-drawn-out battle; where everyone is on guard against everyone else and the police are the common enemy; and where school is generally a place where children are confined by law for so many hours a day, in a state of boredom and resentment. Children are shouted at, cuffed and neglected from birth, not because their parents are wicked but because misery and hopelessness have obliterated the ability to cherish. And the children gang together for support, and look forward to the day when they will be old enough to bully younger ones, in their turn. And yet among all this there is love, and loyalty, and devotion and patience and incredible endurance, and the humour that often shocks more fortunate people. It is still there, this almost indestructible human drive that we call love. The police (with wonderful exceptions) don't believe in it. Nor do most school-teachers. Faced with a class of these children they assume (as older teachers have taught them) that the only way to deal with them is to keep them in the grip of iron discipline, pounce on the least sign of insubordination, and beat any offenders thoroughly. The main aim is to keep order. In between, if possible, a little information may be pumped in. The idealists hope to do more but are too often frightened by the sheer, savage power and energy of the children. They fall back on the stick, not out of ill-will but from failure of nerve, which means failure to love.

There are the good teachers, who love the children, and are loved by them, who actually teach them something. Often enough, half their work is undone by parents who think any interest in school work is 'sissy', who crush rising ambitions with ridicule or a large fist, and take the child from school as soon as the law allows. And behind the teacher is the local authority, the Department of Education and the whole immense bureaucratic structure, who want their lovely buildings to look clean and orderly, and the children to be kept in tidy rows, in the proper places. 'Law and Order' is the slogan of bad government all the world over. In the world of education it means the fear that officials have of anything that might upset the orderliness of the machine that pays them, and gives them their sense of security, importance and power – in fact their identity as people. The spontaneity, ruthless veracity and unorganized emotional reactions of the young are the greatest possible threat to it, and so through the ages the general tendency of bureaucracy (even when made up of friendly, well-meaning people) has been to try to suppress the young by rigid discipline and thorough conditioning, in the attempt to turn them into docile citizens who conform to the models evisaged by the ruling ethos. Children from 'rough' areas are naturally regarded as being especially in need of such suppression, and the success of a school or its head is judged according to whether the school maintains 'law and order'.

All the children who formed the new Risinghill School

when it opened in 1960 came from schools where the repression of the children, by the threat or use of corporal punishment, was taken for granted as a necessity. Many teachers regretted the necessity, many tried to minimize the use of such punishment, but investigation later on showed that there was not a single school in the area, for whatever age-group, which did not use corporal punishment. Basically, most of the teachers, and also the officials behind them, were afraid of the children, for it often happens that such people, emerging from the same kind of background as the children, see in them a symbol of all the vicious, unrespectable tendencies that they themselves have succeeded in repressing or hiding, but not in really transcending. They cannot come to terms with their own 'lower' nature, and the children are their scapegoats. You do not love a scapegoat; love, in fact, was not a thing anyone expected to find as the motive power in running a school. The notion would have been dismissed as at best impractical idealism, at worst neglect of duty and failure of moral courage.

Love, however, was the means by which the new Headmaster of Risinghill intended to run the school. He ran it by love for four years, then it was closed because the officials couldn't stand it any more. No caning, no fear, children laughing, discussing, treating the Head as a friend to be consulted – an end of all dignity, discipline and authority. So they thought, having the same view of authority as the imaginary reporter questioning that mythical Pope. Part of the reason why the officials succeeded in closing Risinghill was that the Headmaster, Mr. Duane, failed to gain the co-operation of all his staff. Many were enthusiastic, but a school in a country with far too few teachers cannot be choosy about its staff. It takes what it can get. Some were the old-fashioned, authoritarian type who felt that any kindness to the children was an abandonment of discipline and order, and who felt outraged and threatened by the new rule of love. Some were confused and weak, and needed guidance and support, and here it seems that Mr. Duane failed by expecting more maturity from them than they could manage. Lacking a strong supporting hand, they turned to those who did give firm, clear (and easily followed) guidance – the authoritarians. Possibly, without this failure to carry his whole staff whole-heartedly into the venture, the London County Council's phobias would have failed to gain a closure. As it was they succeeded, in the face of the protests of parents and neigh-bours, the anguished pleas of the children and the support of much of the press. The record of duplicity, malice, prejudice, lying, bullying and sheer callousness that constitutes the story of how the closure was effected is horrible, but what I want to do here is simply use the record of the reactions of children, staff and others, to give an impression of what the school was like while it was a going concern. All the quotations are from Leila Berg's study of Risinghill, the only one at present available. It is a very perceptive, accurate, though extremely (and rightly) partisan account.

The Headmaster's own remark will do to summarize the nerve-wracking problems of change-over from a régime of coercion (which was all the children had ever known) to one of freedom, co-operation and love.

You go through a period of sheer chaos with each in-coming batch. The children don't believe there's no cane. They have to test your statement. They shout and yell and fight and make life impossible. You have to stand there and let them call you all the four-letter words and every obscenity in the language. You've got to go on talking, and whatever happens keep your temper. It's a nightmare for the teachers and some of them can't take it. I don't blame them. But it's the only way. When the children grasp the fact that there really *isn't* any cane they calm down. In any case they get tired of chaos eventually and then you can start to talk to them as human beings. It works in the end.

Here is a member of the staff remembering some of the difficulties personally experienced:

> I had the idea, as so many do, that if you are simply pleasant, the children will instantly respond. But in that first year, the children didn't; they were very hostile . . . teachers from grammar schools – and people like me – were very hurt. . . . I don't think we were able, most of us, to identify with the children's future, and to know what their adult life was going to be like. . . . Why should teachers expect every child immediately to respond? . . . When the child doesn't, the teacher becomes so hostile that caning follows. It would have been easier with children from good homes. But do we intend to give good education only to children from good homes?

For two terms things got worse, there was gang fighting between members of the original schools and so on. Among other measures to bring peace, Mr. Duane got this discussed at a School Council, and the gangs agreed to bring disputes to the Council for discussion. And little by little the violence stopped. Miss Berg sums up the many small and large reasons why this happened: 'The pupils had creative relationships *demonstrated* to them; they saw the value of them in action, and it made sense.' About this time, a domestic worker in the school had her basket of shopping (food for her family) stolen in the school. Mr. Duane explained to the school that she had spent all her money on it, and her family would have to go hungry. Later, two boys came and told him they'd taken it, and couldn't give it back because they'd eaten it. He gave them some money, told them to go to the market and try to replace each thing that they had taken, as far as they could remember, and quickly. 'Then come back and we'll discuss how you've to refund me.' They paid it all back, out of pocket money. This way they learned concern for others, without lecturing or pressure. They found they were treated as responsible people. They began to relax. They learned the pleasure of books, of open discussion, of being trusted, listened to, appreciated, of making things the way they liked. It wasn't a smooth progress. At first books were things to throw, then they were interesting enough to pinch.

Leila Berg writes: 'The pupils painted fascinating murals, exotic kings and beasts, and things familiar ... a market, a fair, an imaginary Islington park ... so gay, exuberant and witty, proclaiming the flying hopes of the Risinghill children. They hung exquisite wire and tinsel mobiles in the hall ... felt animals, curtains ... decorative wood panels in the library ... (beauty) pervaded the whole school by deliberate policy.' They worked with an artist who came in to help, and created a sculpture from plastic slabs that is now on view at Kenwood (the museum and art collection near London).

A staff-member who had at first been driven desperate by the chaos wrote in 1961: 'The school seems for long periods uncannily quiet ... we have science and art clubs, a canoe club, a school orchestra, choirs and sports teams. The Greek, Turkish and West Indian children sing along with the six other nationalities ... are rehearsing a nativity play ... costumed by the needlework people.' (That play drew resounding applause from the local press, it *used* the varied nationalities instead of ironing them out, it delighted all and was splendid in music, drama, and colour). 'The difficult boys who are due to leave this year have taken their programme of work so seriously that they have cleared a local bomb site and laid out the foundations for a house ... the girls change on Fridays from noisy gigglers to young social workers who visit and help old people ...'

And here are the children's voices:

'Mr. Duane used to treat us lovely, we weren't frightened to go to him when we were in trouble. . . . He was a person you could talk very frankly to. I was at a very strict school before. . . . Risinghill gave me a different outlook on life.'

'It was quite a lovely school because you could learn a lot of things there that would help you when you left . . . I'm a coloured girl, but you could always go to Mr. Duane and talk to him . . . then your mind would feel more at rest. . . . Before, I went to another school . . . you couldn't go to the Headmistress . . . only reason you went to her was to get told off and caned. The teachers . . . didn't sit and listen to your problems. Here a lot of the teachers try to help you. It was good to be at school. . . .'

'. . . all the children in Risinghill School have thought it is very heart-breaking to have it closed. . . .'

'. . . we *enjoyed* working, at Risinghill.'

'. . . they did a marvellous thing at one assembly about slavery and John Brown. It linked up with the colour-bar. The whole of it was read, with music rising in the background and then taking over. . . . If we'd had a whole staff like some of our really first-class senior permanent staff we'd have been fine. . . . My teacher had me at break, dinner-time, any time she could get, to get me through exams. . . . People who put Mr. Duane's policy into practice found it worked.'

'I am grateful to my parents for sending me to Risinghill, I used to hate the coloured people. Now I have many coloured friends.'

A boy painted a picture in the art class and told the teacher it was for him. Then someone offered three pounds for it, the boy was badly off, he could go camping on that. He told the teacher, who said he should sell it. He did – but gave the teacher one pound, and the teacher *took* it: he respected the boy, as the boy liked and trusted him. The boy painted another picture, as a present for him.

Here are the parents: 'I believe Mr. Duane's aim is to make better citizens, and I believe he will do so'. 'The children trusted him ... they regarded him as their friend ... my daughter didn't want to go to any other school, after Risinghill'. 'Mr. Strong gave him special extra classes after school ... this teacher and Mr. Duane gave him every possible encouragement. ... Nothing was too much for him to do for a kid.' 'The whole atmosphere was so *friendly*. They were respectful towards the teachers and yet the teachers were so friendly with them ... you could always go up ... they would explain it to you.' 'What impressed me most was the freedom ...' 'This school is doing something different. They are consulting parents, bringing them into education ....'

Social workers: 'If more schools were like Risinghill we wouldn't have all these children on probation.' 'I saw him in his study ... children came in, staff came in, a grandmother came – he had time for everyone. ... The children laughed, talked, helped me. ... It is all of us who need educating.'

In four years, against rising opposition from the authorities and from a group of teachers in the school, the place became a real community. It was a centre for the district, a place to turn to for help, support, encouragement. It was a centre of art, curiosity, adventure and hope. Parents in such a district are notoriously indifferent to the schools, yet this one had a parent-teacher association that met regularly with attendances up to 200. When closure threatened, it was the parents who rose in rage and fear, held meetings, marched, signed petitions. (It was no use, the decision was made without consulting them, and pushed through against their wishes.) Neighbouring shops and stall-keepers spoke up for the school, the probation officers protested too – even the police. A whole broken down, miserable, *forgotten* neighbourhood, that the authorities wanted to keep quiet so they could go on forgetting it, found meaning and hope and confidence because of four years work in one school, under one man's inspiration. It happened because this man loved the children, and their parents and teachers, and they (many of them) caught it. But it was, after a while, the 'wider community' that came into being that created the setting for the personal relationships that grew up and flourished. Its focus was not the Head, though he symbolized it and made it possible. Its focus was itself, the school, as a forward-moving, living human organism, an expression of the hopes and aims of the people involved. 'Risinghill School' *meant* hope and self-respect and courage and love. And the work of making it welded the community together, because all knew that they had a part to play.

It can be done. This is not an isolated phenomenon, brought about by one irreplaceable man. It shows the conditions under which love can be and actually is politically effective. Herbert Marcuse, philosopher of radical change, describes as one of the basic goals for such change, 'to give sensitivity and sensibility their own right,' which is what education should do if it is education for love.

> These are the qualitatively different features of a free society. . . . They presuppose . . . a type of man who has rid himself of the aggressiveness and brutality that are inherent in the organization of established society, and in their hypocritical puritan morality; a type of man who is biologically incapable of fighting wars and creating suffering; a type of man who has a good conscience of joy and pleasure, and who works, collectively and individually for a social and natural environment in which such an existence becomes possible.

VI

WHAT IS LOVE?

THIS study has so far attempted little systematic analysis of the bewildering variety of motive and experience that comes under the wide heading of 'love'; though there have been interim definitions which made it easier to make some sense of the human behaviour described. The task must now be completed by attempting to draw some kind of conclusions about the nature of this thing called love.

It may seem confusing that up to now at one moment a certain meaning to the word love has been assumed and at another I have queried what was meant by it in certain contexts. But this is how we normally develop an understanding of the meaning of a word. In a most perceptive book on ethics, which studies the relationship between ethics and language sensibility, Herbert McCabe[1] has this passage:

> It is undoubtedly true that the relationship of love to behaviour is complex: I mean we cannot describe what it is like for a man to be loving as easily as we can describe what it is like for a man to be walking. These complications arise, I believe, because 'love' is one of those words whose meaning is constantly expanding for us. I mean by this to contrast it with words like 'jam-jar' or 'perhaps'. We discover at a fairly early age how these words are used, it does not require a great deal of intellectual skill, and a mature, experienced man of sixty will probably be no better at using them than a boy of six. There are, however, other words, and 'love' is one of them, that are much more

[1] HERBERT MCCABE: *Law, Love and Language*, Sheed & Ward 1969.

complicated in their use. We no doubt begin with some fairly simple range of situations in which we can use the word, a fairly narrow range of behaviour that we would think of as loving. Your mother's love seems to consist of being near you, paying attention to you, and giving you what you want. As you grow older you realize that lots of other apparently irrelevant or even apparently hostile acts – like leaving you alone while she cooks your dinner – may be part of a pattern of loving behaviour. . . . 'Love' is thus what we might call a growing word, the whole meaning changes and develops, but this does not in the least imply that it is a vague word, one that might mean almost anything. It is just that a word like 'love' will always have uses that are not constricted by such rules as you have managed to formulate at a particular time. *We can use the word to try to mean more than we could explain at any time.*

My italics, because this shows what I have been trying to do when I applied the word 'love' to the assessment of certain kinds of human situation and, having done so, made certain aspects of the meaning of the word more apparent. I have tried to provide some experience of the meaning of love, both in its presence and its absence, and thereby to enlarge the understanding of it. I have hoped, in this way, to build up in the reader's mind a certain sensitivity to the occurrence of love rather in the way that Herbert McCabe suggests should happen.

It is on this basis that I hope to build an understanding of the meaning of love which is both clearer and more inclusive than our usual use of the word. In order to do this it is necessary to introduce, at this apparently late stage, a very different use of the word 'love' from all those examined so far.

All the examples given so far have shown love happening between people, whether in face-to-face relationships, in groups or in a community so large that most people never meet.

But even in the largest one mentioned, which was London during the 'blitz', there were real face-to-face relationships, and these were an essential part of the 'drive' that took hold of people. There is one more kind of 'drive' which has not been mentioned so far. This is the impulse or emotion described under such headings as 'love of country', or 'love of God'. In the first case, the sentiment referred to is not the same kind of thing as the sharing in a common impulse of generosity and courage which can occur at certain times among large numbers of people. Patriotism may be mixed up with this, but it is not the same thing.

Patriotism can exist even when I dislike most of my countrymen. It is a devotion to something beyond or outside particular persons though it may lead to serving them. In this it has the same character as 'Love of God' which may lead to devotion to people, but is primarily directed beyond them. The lives of saints of all faiths attest that it is often combined with the kind of face-to-face reconciliation already described, but it can exist virtually independently of human contacts. It can be so absorbing that it leaves no room for other concerns, and the most famous mystics have often been of this world-forgetting or even world-denying kind – perhaps because this is so inexplicable to the ordinary person that it attracts attention.

The fact that the phenomenon known as mystical love has been left until this late stage of the book and must now be given a relatively small space in comparison with more familiar aspects of love, is no indication of what I consider to to be its degree of importance, but because at this stage it helps to show up very clearly what is and is not love, and what all the various 'kinds' of love have in common.

Strangely linked to the idea of mystical love is the realm of anti-love, the forces of hate and destruction. The link lies in the fact, already clear in many different contexts in this book, that what happens to love depends very greatly on how people are taught to think about it. As I noticed in the description of Balinese methods of child-care, the drive to love which is totally frustrated, rather than diverted or modified, finds outlets which are very far from loving. The same thing could be seen in the description of exploitative sex in eighteenth-century London, where a social group was deprived by custom and education of all opportunity to love. The need to 'break out' and 'go further' could not be shifted, it took the only available forms, created its own 'doctrines' of the pursuit of pleasure, and the results were hideous.

Mystical desire, similarly, needs to define its object rightly if it is to develop as love. When people are moved by mystical aspirations whose symbolic objects are their own racial identity, or personal or group power whether political or magical – or even 'the people', and 'the country' when conceived as a quasi-divinity – in such cases the results are evil, the emotions generated are hate, lust and revenge. Even such things as 'art' and 'science', if they are allowed to become gods, can lead to horrible acts against human beings.

Storm Jameson puts the tragic problem movingly in her introduction to the famous *Diary of Ann Frank*, in which the Jewish girl in hiding from the Nazis records her lonely growth towards womanhood. Knowing as we do that she was to end her brief life in the concentration camp at Belsen, the diary reads as an extraordinary testament to the indestructibility of love. Storm Jameson puts it in a wide human context:

> It is strengthening, a humbling experience, to watch this child, this young girl, come so far, unfold so richly, in little more than two years. . . . Let us press just for a moment on the feeling of stupefaction that must start in us when we think that, in our lifetime, side by side with the amazing achievements of scientists . . . there exist these vast slaughterhouses for human beings, and that, to a number of her fellow human beings, to send Ann Frank to one of them seemed

a natural thing to do. . . . What moves a man to feel such contempt for his fellow human beings that he comes to believe that a Jew or a political opponent may, must, be treated as vermin and stamped out?

A doctrine moved him. Men learned early how to press a doctrine over ears and eyes, so that they could torture without being distracted by the victim's agony. . . . The human reason is able to justify any cruelty by showing that it is necessary, part of a process, a term in a majestic logic – and the rest of it. . . . Why did the Germans bring about the death of this charming, intelligent, good child? Because they had convinced themselves that they had the right, that in destroying her they furthered aims, a future, they had decided to realize. . . . Dying, of hunger and misery, in Belsen Ann Frank took with her into a mass grave every exquisite intellectual structure which allows its servants to torture, to work to death, to kill, for an idea.

For a little over two years this child worked on herself, with tears, patience, gaiety, with all the energy of a quick mind and a will turned towards goodness. She taught herself a smile of happiness and faith. In all humility, we can, surely, believe that this smile, this profound smile, was not lost, even in Belsen, even if she could no longer hold out against the arrogance of men without God.

This passage makes a dramatic contrast between the goodness and love of the Jewish teenager and the hideous evil of the ideology that killed her. 'Men without God', the author calls them, but the real horror of this contrast lies in the fact that they were *not* men without God, or at least not men without *a* god. They had a god, who absorbed all their devotion – his name was Arianism and Hitler was his prophet. Through history, persecutors and torturers have had their god, and done their work all the more effectively in his name, whether that happened to be Moloch, Jahweh, Christ, the People, the State, Freedom, or Law and Order. Would it be altogether untrue to say that those who served such gods with zeal and dedication *loved* their god?

The tentative definitions of love given so far would in fact cover both notions. If it can be described as some sort of drive towards, or desire for, a wider, deeper, more important 'beyond' in human life, this can be made to include an impulse that involves the whole-hearted crushing and killing of all that stands in the way, as well as the impulse that overcomes obstacles both in the person and in his circumstances and flowers into joy, compassion and hope.

Yet there is something wrong. Maybe the definition can include both, but we can't leave it at that. One experiences a revulsion at the idea that Ann Frank and her killers can be set side by side, on an equal basis, as examples of people motivated by love. It is like saying that the Christian Eucharist and the Black Mass are really the same kind of thing, or that de Sade's experiments are morally on a level with the passion of Romeo and Juliet. Yet in these pairs it can truly be said that both, in each case, are searching for the 'beyond', the 'further reaches' of human experience. Both are convinced that there is more to life than they can normally experience, and both desire that 'more'.

If we judge one better than the other, or deny to one the title of 'love', what is the standard of judgement that we have used, perhaps unconsciously?

The insights of the mystics are a help at this point, partly because their 'disembodied' love is, from *one* point of view, closest to the equally 'disembodied' love that leads to actions like those of a Himmler or a de Sade. Their love is directed not primarily at human beings but at something 'beyond'. But the way they feel about human beings is evidently rooted in this same impulse.

Out of the vast store of the outpourings of human love in its search for the final truth which it desires I have chosen a very few little passages. First of all are passages in which the mystic is discovering, or teaching, what seems to be necessary if the soul is to love truly. All these voices, of whatever faith, speak as one, and all speak from profound personal experience.

Here is the voice of the anonymous Canon of Frankfurt who wrote the *Theologia Germanica*:

> Where men are enlightened with the true light, they perceive that all which they might desire or choose is nothing to that which all creatures, as creatures, ever desired or chose to know.... Nevertheless, there remaineth in them a desire to go forward and get nearer to the Eternal Goodness; that is, to come to clearer knowledge, and warmer love, and more comfortable assurance and perfect obedience and subjection; so that every enlightened man could say: 'I would fain be to the Eternal Goodness what his own hand is to a man'. And he feareth always that he is not enough so, and longeth for the salvation of all men. And such men do not call this longing their own, nor take it unto themselves, for whatsoever is good shall no one take unto himself as his own, seeing that it belongeth to the eternal goodness only.

This passage recalls the one with which this book began, in which Socrates reflected on the desire for truth, the ultimate beauty which is reality itself, for it is only then that a man can 'bring forth reality'. He does not have it of his own will but must find it in the divine beauty. Blessed John Tauler, talking about 'peace of the soul' is evidently saying the same thing. This 'peace' is very like Socrates' 'beauty', and the 'good' which the Canon of Frankfurt says belongs to the Eternal Goodness only. Here is John Tauler's warning to his disciples:

> Children, it is in this self-departure, this going forth from self-will, that the essential peace of soul is born in us.... Believe me, that essential peace never comes otherwise....

Men wise in their own conceit will bid you do this and do that to become perfect – and it is all a set of observances of their own contrivance.

From a time nearer our own comes the voice of Léon Bloy, struggling to express the same sense that real love can only work in one way:

I had the deep feeling – I am deeply distressed not to be able to express it – that there is but one help. It is the absolute gift of oneself, such as Jesus practised it. One must allow oneself to be buffeted, spat upon, scourged, crucified – All else is vanity.

It is the same knowledge that Ann Frank was groping for – self-willed, clever, Ann, greedy for life, wanting things her own way, yet struggling to understand the others and appreciate them, to see the good in them, to give herself, finding courage and peace in the sky and the trees she could see through the window, in Peter, the boy she was learning to love, and in God.

I think about 'the good' of going into hiding, of my health, and with my whole being of the 'dearness' of Peter, of that which is still embryonic and impressionable and which neither of us dare to name or touch, of that which will come some time: love, the future, happiness, and 'the beauty' which exists in the world . . . he who has courage and faith will never perish in misery.

Yet she knew that many suffered and died, and that it might happen to her, that this might be part of what she was looking for.

Be brave! Let us remain aware of our task and not grumble. . . . God has never deserted our people. Right through the ages there have been Jews, through all the ages they have had to suffer, but it has made them strong, too.

For her, love, future, happiness and suffering were mixed, and to all of them she had to learn to give herself, though her natural impulse was to assert her rightness and guard what she knew as good and desirable, regardless of others.

The human struggle for 'the good', for 'beauty', 'peace' or 'happiness' is the theme of so much poetry and of the writings of all mystics. The Hindu mystical poet Rabindranath Tagore writes yet again about the one essential condition of the attainment of the good. He, speaking for so many, knows what love means.

> Time after time I came to your gate
> with raised hands, asking for more and yet more.
> You gave and gave, now in slow
> measure, now in sudden excess.
> I took some, and some things I let
> drop; some lay heavy on my hands;
> Some I made into playthings and broke
> them when tired; till all the wrecks and
> the hoards of your gifts grew immense,
> hiding you, and the ceaseless expectation
> wore my heart out.
>
> Take, oh take – has now become my cry.
> Shatter all from this beggar's bowl:
> put out this lamp of the importunate
> watcher, hold my hands, raise me from
> the still-gathering heap of your gifts
> into the bare infinity of your uncrowded presence.

This is perhaps the clearest statement of the difference for which we are looking. But all these lovers of God (or the Infinite, or the Self, or the One – and these are only a few of his many names) are saying very clearly: you can tell genuine love because it opens out and gives itself, it seems to grow by being part of that which is the All, the Beloved. You can recognize false 'love' because it encloses itself, and seeks to grow by grabbing and snatching and keeping. Here is the modern mystic, Thomas Merton, a man very much of our time, a man who knew how to love, describing those who have reached perfect self-giving in mystical love:

> They are the only ones who will ever be able to enjoy life altogether. They have renounced the whole world as it has been given into their possession. They alone appreciate the world and the things that are in it. They are the only ones capable of understanding joy. Everybody else is too weak for joy. Joy would kill anybody but these weak. They are the clean of heart. They see God. He does their will, because his will is their own. . . . Their freedom is without limit, they reach out to comprehend our misery and drown it in the tremendous expansion of their own innocence, that washes the world with its light.

As Socrates says, 'Would that be an ignoble life?' But the condition is a 'going out', an 'emptying', and this is the dividing line. On the one side, as Tagore says, 'the wrecks and the hoards – grew immense' hiding what is really desired, the wrecks of lives destroyed by doctrines of self-exaltation, in the name of a god whose name is not love. There is no joy here. On the other side 'the bare infinity of your crowded presence', crowded with people to be loved and a world to be appreciated and enjoyed, because it is not exploited by the pseudo-love whose motive is the fear of annihilation and the need to increase and increase.

Because of the universal pressure of this fear the way of love is hard, and the various Buddhist schools of thought have realized and mapped the difficulty of it more thoroughly than most. An English writer[1] sums it up, and sums up also the witness of seekers of all faiths, as he points out why that hard way is worthwhile: 'For the Way is long and arduous. Yet

[1] CHRISTMAS HUMPHREYS: *Buddhism*, Penguin.

in the end the self lies dead, and the Self, the expanding individual consciousness, is merged in that "Suchness of the Heart" or Bodhi-citta, which is all-Love, all-Wisdom and all else'.

Mystical love, peculiar as it seems to our culture, does provide us with the touchstone we needed. For real love is not only the desire for the 'other' or 'beyond' in human life and experience, it is the impulse to give oneself to that 'otherness'. The attempt to possess is anti-love, the nearest thing to the devil that we can envisage, and the mystics see it clearly. There is a good reason why mystics can do this with more assurance than other kinds of lovers; the genuine fruition of their experience, as such, depends on the willingness to 'let go', to 'go out of oneself' or whatever phrase is used. Whereas other styles of loving can often find substitutes for the real thing which are pleasant and satisfactory, the false mystic does not attain to the contemplation of the Beloved. He has to fall back on impressing other people to get a little glory and prestige, or on the thrill of persecution, even of himself. This is anti-love, and every treatise on prayer has its warnings against fake mystics, or against self-love and the pursuit of pleasure, even in prayer.

But it is not easy to draw the boundary in actual human experience. In human love (and that includes mystical love) there is a mixture of anti-love as well, and this is the torture and burden of the mystic who knows, as others do not, that this is *the* barrier to pure truth and knowledge. But the standard of judgement is still a useful one, because it helps us to detect fake gods whose service is anti-love. Patriotism or the worship of some other tribal symbol is a cover that can be used to demand anti-love from people. The Germans allowed themselves to be drawn to worship the god of racial superiority and sacrifice millions of lives to him, as well as their own integrity. Christians tortured and destroyed each other in honour of Christ, who was for them the symbol of their own spiritual greed and envy. But patriotism, or some other religious emotion, can motivate people like Edith Cavell, Thomas More, Elizabeth Fry, Albert Schweitzer and Dorothy Day.

This real mystical love shows up more clearly the nature of 'everyday' love. It has provided me with a useful definition, but the only point of the definition is that it refers us to something we can check by experience and respond to in real life. Because mystical love attaches itself to something which is beyond the human it is easier to see that *all* love actually reaches further than the human object. Love that stops short at its human object is liable to become anti-love, because it depends on the existence of its object *as lovable*, that is, as a sort of object of worship. Therefore it must, if necessary, *force* the beloved to go on being *there* and to go on being lovable. He or she (or they, or the Cause) must continue to have those qualities that the lover needs to find, and if, in reality, they begin to change, or never were there at all, the lover increasingly tries to make them exist, or pretends that they exist. The possessive mother wants a dependent child to cherish. She tries to keep the adult dependent, and prevent him going away. The founder of some useful work after a certain point may try desperately to prevent its further expansion or change to meet new needs, because then it would no longer be *his*. The same applies to people who have made their life work round some institution and can't face any alteration, to a husband whose wife was once in need of his support and who cannot allow her to stand on her own feet and be herself, to a devoted teacher who feels bitter because a favourite pupil will not follow the academic career she planned for him. So the love that takes its immediate object as its god – that is, its goal and medium and motive – easily becomes anti-love. It may destroy the beloved and it certainly warps the lover.

But love that reaches beyond its objects, however good, a love whose motive and impulse are bigger than any immediate good, can continue even if its immediate object changes, fails or goes away. This is true even when the lover does not consciously have anything in mind but the person or cause that he or she loves. One can see it in action. The man who has made a school where there is love and trust and life can see his work grow beyond him, can see himself superseded and set aside, without bitterness because it is not the achievement he loves, but the life and love he has set free in the children. That is what matters – the place and the methods and even the stated ideals are only means. The wife who continues to love a man who turns out to be weak, selfish or unfaithful loves what is real in him, his human self, and does not stop at the collection of qualities that might be satisfactory to herself. These are only two very common examples which show that love which is genuine has to be bigger than its apparent object or 'focus'.

It may seem that something so rarified as mystical love must be altogether too drained of ordinary human emotion to help much in learning to recognize the quality of inter-personal love, and that even when love is 'bigger' than its immediate object or focus it is at least reassuringly imaginable and attainable. Mystics are suspect for being too detached. The stories of the Buddha record his infinite patience and gentleness with people who came to him, and this we can admire, but most of us are harried by violent emotions. Must there be such utter detachment before there can be real love?

Detachment can be a selfish, arrogant anti-love, seeking personal liberation and esoteric experience. This is not the detachment of the true mystic which, whether quiet and gentle or violent and passionate, simply means that willing-ness to give oneself which is the work of genuine love. Detachment means the refusal to be attached to anything

that might hinder that self-giving. It will not cling on, guard
or hoard. The extraordinary records of mystical love show
very clearly that this special manifestation of love is a way of
realizing the truth of love, but there is more than that. It also
shows that love is not, in reality, divided into different 'species'
as if human beings in love were a zoo in which separate areas
might be labelled 'sexual love', 'parental love', 'philanthropy',
'mysticism', 'patriotism 'and so on. It shows that love is one,
the vital human impulse towards completeness and freedom.

Compare these groups of passages, three on parting, two
on union:

> O noble eagle, O sweet lamb!
> O blaze of fire, kindle me!
> One hour is too long for me
> One day is like a thousand years
> If you should be remote from me
> No more than a week and a day.
> In Hell I should prefer to stay
> Where I already am
> When God is alien to the loving soul
> That is pain beyond death,
> And pain beyond all pain.

> Deare, I dye
> As often as from thee I goe,
> Though it be but an hour agoe,
> And lovers hours be full eternity.

> Sick with love, with ailing heart
> Pain, dullness and bitter smart
> Kept me too long apart
> From my dearest Lord

> This Extasie doth unperplex
> (We said) and tell us what we love, ...
> Love, these mixt soules, doth mixe againe,

And makes both one, each this and that . . .
When love, with one another so
Interinanimates two soules
That abler soule which thence doth flow,
Defects of lonelinesse controules.
Wee then, who are this new soule, know
Of what we are compos'd and made,
For, th' Atomies of which we grow,
Are soules, whom no change can invade.

When through love the soul goes beyond all working of the intellect and all images in the mind, and is rapt above itself, utterly leaving itself, it flows into God: then is God its peace and fullness. It loses itself in the infinite solitude and darkness of the Godhead; but so to lose itself is rather to find itself.

Whether in the anguish of parting, or in the discovery of a union which yet creates the self more perfectly, these lovers are clearly describing experiences that have the same human character. Whether the object be human or divine, if either is love, both are love. The same thing is going on in both cases. It is not a new observation that sexual love and mystical love use the same language, and one can argue for ever about whether this means that mysticism is 'nothing but' sublimated sex, or sexual love is 'really' an experience of the divine. What matters is that here is the human experience of love. Whether the voice be that of the thirteenth-century German, Mechtild of Magdeburg, the sixteenth-century Frenchman Louis de Blois, the seventeenth-century metaphysical Englishman John Donne, or the twentieth-century French/English/American Thomas Merton the testimony is to the power of love in human life. And its reality as love, not pseudo-love or anti-love, is made plain by that self-giving, open and generous character which mystics of all ages and faiths have discerned as the acid test of genuineness.

The influence of Freud, or rather of ill-understood versions of his teaching, has made it common for people afraid of love to discuss it as 'nothing but sex' in various forms. The notion that a child's devotion to his mother, a brother's to his brother, a friend's to his friend, a citizen's to his city, or a mystic's to God are all examples of sexual drives variously deflected is similar to the notion – whose origin is in the same school of psychology – that anyone who acts as support and symbol to another human being in his struggle towards maturity is a 'mother figure' or 'father figure'. It is a perfectly useful clinical description, as long as we can also turn the proposition upside down, and see the mother and father as the first and most usual supports and guides, and genital sexuality as the most easily identified, usual and absorbing manifestation of the human impulse tentatively called love. Earlier in the book I suggested that it would help to get our ideas straight if we could make the effort to think of, for instance, mothers as sister or wife substitutes for small children. Equally it is a help in sorting out our ideas about the nature of love in general if we can learn to think of sexual love as, say, a genital type of brother and sister devotion, or a private type of patriotism, or individualized mysticism. All these descriptions can be truthfully applied to the sexual relationship, and illuminate it, just as the other relationships in their turn were illuminated by Freud's insight into their links with the sexual one. To make these comparisons is helpful in enlarging our understanding of each one. The mistake is to regard any one as *including* all the others, and reducing them to it. So, as we should not say that the bonds of love in a religious community are 'nothing but' the children's need for a mother to lean on, so we should not say that the mystic's longing for God is 'nothing but' distorted sexual desire or that the bride's desire for her bridegroom is 'nothing but' a concealed need for God. There is a great deal of overlapping in the kinds of emotions and experiences that make up all the kinds of relationships mentioned in this book. What they have in common is this thing called love, and it has a constant quality which, when pointed out, can be recognized anywhere. It is enormously powerful, breaking down barriers of convention, law, custom and self-will. It can overcome all the ingenious methods devised by the human fear of it. It is the most basic human need, at the level of life at which human beings are able to be human, because their energies are not entirely absorbed by the need to keep alive. And once love has begun to grow in a person even the pressures of sheer necessity cannot always destroy it. In times of famine, plague and devastation some men throw in their humanity and prey on each other in a way animals never do. But others seem to find in these circumstances the final liberation of love. Those who remembered Ann Frank in Belsen – shaven, emaciated and naked – said that her face was 'radiant' with love and courage.

The sheer force of love remains astonishing, even though myths through the ages have affirmed its supreme importance. Cupid and Psyche, Tristan and Isolde, Romeo and Juliet, Tony and Maria of *West Side Story* – the doomed lovers – are the salvation of the hard-hearted. In all these tales the lovers, as the mystics teach, must 'go out' of the normal and the everyday, into unknown regions of danger. And the way they follow, looking for love, may lead to what seems an actual denial of love. It is this fact that finally makes it clear that love itself is 'bigger' than those it embraces, serves, lifts up and transforms. The terrible conflicts of truly loving people are a witness to the ruthless demand that love makes on people who allow themselves to listen.

There is the strange story of the Spanish girl Casilda de Padilla, engaged to a man she deeply loved, who was assailed by a conviction that she should go to the convent. She battled against the feeling, for she asked no better than to spend her life with the man she loved. But it was too strong. Twice she ran away from home to the convent, and finally her family allowed her to stay.

There is Franz Jagerstetter, the Austrian peasant who, against the advice of all his family, friends, clergy, refused military service to the Nazis because he considered their régime immoral and their war unjust. He died rather than serve the evil cause, although he had a wife and children whom he loved and who might well suffer through his refusal to go against his conscience. He is only one among many who have died rather than deny the truth, though it meant leaving beloved children, husbands or wives.

'I would have liked to spare you the pain and sorrow you must bear because of me' he wrote to his wife just before his death, 'but you know we must love God even more than family. The (military) oath would not be a lie for someone who believes he can go along . . . but if I know I cannot . . . obey everything I would promise . . . then I would be guilty of a lie. . . . It is still best that I speak the truth, even if it costs me my life . . . if someone argues from the standpoint of family, do not be troubled, for it is not permitted to lie, even for the sake of the family. If I had ten children the greatest demand upon me would still be the one I must make of myself'.

This demand is the call of the 'something more' but in such cases it is not in the least pleasant and attractive. It is simply a demand that has to be obeyed. It can present itself as the demand of God, of country, of a cause, or of love for another human being. It is the demand which will compel the devotion of a Mother Teresa to the dying in the slums of Calcutta, of a Danilo Dolci who gave up the prospects of a brilliant marriage and career to marry a peasant and serve the poor of Sicily. It drives young and old, lovers and parents and children, people of all religions and none. You can call it what you like, to suit the circumstance, but the character of this demand identifies it, as the mystics have shown. It is the demand to 'leave all things', to 'go out', to 'give oneself'. There can be as many descriptions as there are cases, but they are all seized by the same power.

Power? Drive? Impulse? Demand? Such words have occurred because they seemed appropriate to describe what was going on. They suggest, however, that not only is love 'bigger' than the focus or object to which it attaches itself, and 'bigger' than the lover himself – but it is also 'bigger' in that it does not originate in the lover nor is it under his control. He is, almost literally, seized by it. Yet he is seized because there is that in him which finds it hard to resist the demand. It can do so, but if it does the person is partly destroyed.

Love, then, is an impulse arising out of the very fabric of personality. You could even say it *makes* the person, for one who is responsive to the demands can actually be seen growing into the person he is capable of being, but would not otherwise have been. But love does not arise spontaneously, it arises in response to something else. When we say someone is responsive in this sense we mean they react lovingly to situations that demand love. Yet love does not 'reside' in the lover, for, as we have seen, genuine love breaks down barriers between people, and draws them out of themselves towards others, but also and at the same time towards 'something more'. It is a *shared* discovery, therefore, of the otherness of human life, and it is of its nature to be shared, for even the solitary mystic, if he is a genuine mystic, is opening himself to 'the All-Love, the All-Wisdom and all else'.

This is probably as far as it is possible to go in the discussion of love without entering into realms of specialist interpretation, which means describing love according to a particular set of doctrines about human life, whether religious or not.

Although I have drawn my examples of loving and non-loving thought and behaviour from many cultures and religions I have tried to display it in terms of human experience which can be verified by the reader if he wishes. I have not always been able to do this, for a study of the strange phenomena of love sometimes demands a description which goes beyond the immediately verifiable if it is to make sense at all, and this is why I called on mystics of several faiths to do the describing for me. But further than this I cannot go without the use of theological or ideological words which tie down the description to a particular interpretation of the facts.

This is not to say that such an interpretation should not be made. On the contrary, it is most important that the task of interpretation should be undertaken, and in another context I have undertaken it myself. My own type of interpretation can, in fact, be discerned in much that I have written here, and I make no apology for this. Whoever undertook this kind of task would be bound to have some sort of systematic view of the material, and this would appear. But to take the interpretation further and more explicitly would go beyond the scope of this kind of study, which tries to present the material in such a way that, though the author's own opinions are not concealed, the reader may set them aside if he wishes and reach different conclusions on the evidence given. I can only add that I hope he will not.

To end the book I want to present the final witness of three odd little stories, all true and all from the recent past, which throw considerable light on the nature of love.

The first is an incident reported by Laurenz Van der Post, who knows Japan well, writing in a Sunday newspaper. He tells how on a recent visit he met a Japanese girl with two foreign men. The girl was clearly distressed, and the visitor, knowing the language, asked if he could help her. She explained that the two men took her for a prostitute. 'And' she said, 'it is true. I am a prostitute. But today is Sunday'. On Sundays it was her custom, she said, to take a bath of purification, to worship at the shrine, to walk in the country and enjoy the pleasure of flowers and natural things. In the evening she also attended concerts of French music, of which she was very fond. 'During the week I am a machine' she concluded. 'On Sunday I am *myself*, Jewel' (this was her name). The two foreigners were impressed. They apologized, bowed, and sent her home in a taxi at their expense. This little story is revealing. In the mouth of one intelligent and sensitive girl, who naturally did not regard her professional activities as morally reprehensible, we have an exact description of the reason why the exploitation of impersonal sex is an unlikely setting for love. However much fun is had, the body is being treated impersonally, it is 'a machine' for pleasure, and release, or revenge or self-assertion, or the satisfaction of any number of a large range of psychological needs. It is not a personal communication. 'On Sunday I am *myself*', not because she dispenses with sex but because she is using her whole self to feel, to discover, to worship, to enjoy. The revulsion from impersonal 'machine' sex often leads to the feeling that the price of being 'myself' is indeed the rejection of sex, and this is one of the reasons for the long emphasis on virginity, chastity and self-control. There are other, ignoble reasons, but this one is present, even in the same person. So, for instance, we find that medieval saints, sex-obsessed and devoted to wild extremes of asceticism as some of them were, were also capable of a gentle, tender and deep affection for a number of people, as well as a spontaneous and undemanding compassion for the many in need whom they met and helped.

But practical compassion is difficult, and it is easier to deal with human misery by rule, under cover of compassion. The next story, repeated by Kathleen Whitehorn in the London

Observer, shows the attempt to suppress love by applying 'humane' rules instead, and what happens to people when their love is denied. It also shows that a stupid and brutal system can sometimes employ people whom it has not yet succeeded in brutalizing. Here is the report, written up from a T.V. programme on the subject:

A woman was found wandering drunk and homeless one night with her baby boy, who was then placed under a fit person order [this means his mother was not considered a 'fit person' to care for him] and taken into care. After a few months her situation had so improved that the children's department reckoned that the baby could go home to his mother on trial, especially as he was not doing well in the nursery.

Unfortunately she was then turned out of her room, the department lost touch with her for six weeks; when they found her again the child-care officers recommended that the boy now be left with his mother, but on the advice of its Chairman, Alderman X, the children's committee paid more attention to a medical report on the *area* (not her room) and said the child was to go. Two child-care officers went to collect him and simply couldn't bring themselves to do it; there seemed no reason that the mother could understand. 'You can't just walk into someone's home and just say you're taking the baby without any reason', she said.

But taken he finally was, by child-care officers who were tougher and senior. Without the baby, the mother had a breakdown. The children's department hauled her out of that and found her another room. So little confidence in the baby's return did . . . the child-care officer concerned with the case have that she resigned to make the T.V. programme about it. Ten days before the T.V. programme and the day before a solicitor they had hired for the mother was due to apply to the courts to have the 'fit person' order revoked, the baby was given back. The timing, say the Council, was sheer coincidence.

There are too many morals in this tale to unpack in detail and there are too many tales like it to make that necessary. But it brings the problems and queries raised in this book right up to date and puts them inescapably under our noses. A few of the questions it raises are, why is well established knowledge about the way children develop emotionally ignored by those who make rules for their welfare? What is the significance of the horrid little fact that the 'tougher' children's officers were also 'senior'? Do we even begin to understand what it does to human personality to be deprived of the beloved? There is a morass of misery and official callousness summed up in the phrase 'without the baby, the mother had a breakdown'. It raises questions about conflict of loyalties – the child or the Council who pays you? – similar to Franz Jagerstetter's, but almost in reverse. This story needs to be pondered. What kind of a society do we live in that allows a child's future to be decided on the basis of hygiene rather than love, and in which the 'tough' officers who are less affected by love, are the ones who get promoted? If you think about love at all it is not allowable to keep it inside the covers of a book. If you let yourself respond to it, it demands that you judge, and act on your judgement.

Finally, here is a story from a book by someone who did judge and did act. She did not act in her own country, which may seem odd, for no one who takes an unprejudiced look at contemporary America can imagine that she could not have found need or poverty and misery in many parts of the U.S. just as profound as in Southern Italy. But to Italy she went, and after all it really isn't important where you go, provided you love. She went to work in a squalid little hillside town in the Abruzzi, whose crumbling houses were full of hungry, apathetic, superstitious and suspicious people. The book's author, Ann Cornelisen, and a friend, set up a nursery school in the town after overcoming much opposition. There the

children were fed, learned to play games and enjoy themselves. The school was free, but the mothers were told that the
children must come to school clean, or they would be sent
home again. Arising out of this reasonable rule, one story
deserves to be recorded almost in full in spite of the author's
rather old-fashioned 'missionary' attitude to the limited
imagination and outlook of the run-down culture she (so
understandably) disliked and despised.

One child I felt we had to take was Giovanna, a tall
scrawny girl of five with fine delicate features and eyes as
blue as the Mediterranean. She was next youngest of four
children of the *villaggio* whore. . . . They wandered through
the streets, abandoned, meek, dirty little things whose only
sin in life was stealing food.

The first morning Giovanna came to the nursery she was
mute, but her eyes sparkled with curiosity and joy. She
wanted to do everything, see everything, touch everything.
When anyone came near her she cringed away and hid her
head, but she peeked from under her arm with those
twinkling eyes. Never a word. We let her alone, tried to
include her as normally as possible. I went to talk to her
mother about cleaning her up. Her hair was long and
matted, her clothes stank, but it was the mother's fault, not
Giovanna's. Before I got in the house she was screaming at
me: 'You can't send her home . . . you got to keep her now.
Isn't my fault she wets her bed. You took her, you keep
her.'

One morning I took Giovanna in the kitchen with me
and sat down to talk to her. She leaned against my knees
peering into my eyes with such intensity I was afraid she
did not understand what I was saying. Chichella, our cook,
came over to squat beside her.

We three went off to the bathroom for our session with
D.D.T., scissors and soap. Giovanna radiated joy like the
heat from an electric fire. She did not complain about the
D.D.T. that stung her scalp and got in her eyes. Combing

the snarls was fun. Chichella and I made questioning faces behind her back. Something was very wrong . . . and then maybe we both realized at the same time . . . that little girl had never had so much attention, so much love spent on her in her life. We could have cut off her leg so long as we did something for and to her. When it was over and she was deloused, cut, washed, combed and more or less dry she said her first word.

'When do we wash it again?'

'But, cara mia, it's up to you to keep it clean now. You come show me a week from now if you've kept it this clean.' She was smiling at herself in the mirror.

'I will, I will', and she threw her arms around my neck.

I have found her washing her hair at the fountain with yellow laundry soap and I have admired the scalloped cuts she gives herself; her hair has never been dirty or lousy again. It was a sapphire-eyed peacock who went back into the room with the other children that day; she knew she was special and especially loved, and I think that sense of being loved has stayed with her.

The end of the story is that love is not enough. Her older brother raped her. The nuns at San Fortunato took her in, have kept her and have been as kind as they know how to be, but they chill my blood when they speak of her in her presence as 'Our little Giovanna, who was molested by her brother.'

She is 12 now, bright in school, beautiful with a strong, solemn beauty, and a few months ago I heard that an older couple wanted to take her into their home, which meant she would be their servant, but safe and perhaps loved. When the nuns told me about it, she was with me holding my hand timidly as she did so many years ago. This might be her chance, I thought, but just last week I heard she had been sent back to the convent because she still wets her bed and the older couple lost patience with her. I know no answer except love and expert care, but Torre Greca can offer neither to Giovanna, I am afraid.

'We could have cut off her legs so long as we did something for her and to her.' That is scarcely an exaggeration. That is how much human beings need to be loved, and need to love, and that is how the capacity to love can survive the most appalling conditions if it is given half a chance. It was, in fact, more like a quarter of a chance, and the story ends on a question. We don't know what will happen to Giovanna. Maybe she'll end up like her mother, but it seems unlikely she will ever become really unloving. 'The sense of love has stayed with her'. Once awakened, it takes a lot to kill it. And I like the last, sad comment: 'I know no answer except love and expert care'. This brings out an aspect of the study of love which I mentioned earlier and which is too often forgotten. Miss Cornelisen puts 'love and expert care' side by side. She knows both are necessary, and one alone will not do. But perhaps this putting side by side begs the question. The point is that love without as expert a care as is available is not love in the fullest sense. Real love is effective. If you really love you do something about it, and do it as well as you can manage to learn how, whether the technique be that of prayer, nursing, sex, child-care or revolution. Perhaps the most succesful anti-love device of our clever culture has been this separation of love from technique. To put them together has been made to seem almost blasphemous, it is one of those taboos by which a society prevents people from doing things that might undermine its values, without actually giving them a reason not to.

The reason for this taboo is that if we once learned to link love and technique our culture would come apart at the seams, and an entirely new one would begin to grow in its place. For centuries, we have been confusing love with the privacy of emotional responses, where it is ineffective except as a domestic cement or a mildly reformative social force. Possibly this book may have helped to show that it is more than that, and here these three little incidents each in their own way underline the evil of this particular sin against love. The separation of technique from love in sex produces the 'machine' that is the prostitute. The separation of technique from love produces the type of child-care that puts cleanliness above love and can set aside the pain of mother and child as officially irrelevant. The separation of technique and love produces the *laissez-faire* government that 'allows' towns like Torre Greca to exist, the kindly ineffectiveness of the nuns who could not help Giovanna and never realized that more was demanded by love; and even the exasperated pity of the American girl who could regard their ineptitude as inevitable, and unalterable. Nothing in human society is unalterable if once we can marry love to technique and absolutely refuse to allow divorce or even separation. And technique means know-how, accurate knowledge – in other words a right doctrine about how human beings are. In all the aspects of human life and society that I have described which destroy or distrust love it is done because people teach, and learn, an anti-love doctrine about what people are like and how they develop.

Our culture is a curious mixture. One of its components is the Judaeo-Christian tradition filtered through Greek abstractionism and Roman practicality (the Romans being among the most expert at enforcing a separation between technique and love). We have now virtually outgrown the Christian bit, in its Greek-coloured version, though a number of preconceptions survive. We are far enough, now, beyond the first rejections of traditional Christianity for a non-Christian culture to be able to look at early Christian writings without irrelevant emotions either of distaste or of reverence. It is therefore becoming possible to begin to recover the unique Jewish understanding of human nature, which the early Christian teaching took up and 'unpacked' in new and less traditional terms.

If we are seriously concerned to understand the extraordinary force in human life called love we could do worse than take another look at the startling insights of that excitable, exasperating intellectual, Paul of Tarsus. I have tried to show, in this book, how universal and powerful love is in shaping human life; the elaborate precautions, both conscious and unconscious, which have been taken to prevent its influence show this more clearly than anything else could. Love is not just a power, it is the fundamental impulse, the spirit of man itself, in its activity. This is why it matters that it should be given its best chance, and that chance comes by the union of love and technique – love in action, in fact. The idea was normal to the Jews even if they often failed to maintain the union. Paul took it up, and hammered at it. I propose to end this book as I began it, with a quotation from a great man's work. Socrates showed what man might desire and called the desire of it, love. Paul believed also that love is to be sought, but he was sure that it can be attained because it is not only ahead of us, to be sought, but also in us, in our bodily selves. Therefore the search for it is also its manifestation. Love is the way we seek for love. In order to bring out this aspect of his thinking, which concerns the subject of this study, what follows is a very free rendering of his words, in terms which make their relevance clearer than his particular choice of terms (suited to his Roman readers) is able to do for us:

I appeal to you, my brothers, remembering what love has actually achieved in you, to consider your whole selves, body and soul, as offered and given over to the service of love. Do not accommodate yourselves to the ideas of a greedy and materialistic world, but change yourselves by renewing your thinking and feeling in such a way as to discover what is really right for human beings, what is good and fitting and fully human.

And since I have learned much in this way myself, I feel

bound to tell you what I know about such a life. You should not allow yourself to have an inflated notion of your importance. Judge yourself in a detached and sensible way, to discover what kind of work you should undertake in this service of love. For as there are many parts in a human body, but they don't all have the same function, so we are all members of one body and each of us belongs to all the others. If we all have different skills, according to our particular abilities and gifts, let us make use of this variety. If somebody is a thinker or preacher, let him do that work as well as he is able to. If someone's gift is for caring for people, let him get on with it. If it is for teaching, let him teach, if it is for public relations or counselling, let him do that. If you are in a position to help others financially, do it generously and thoroughly, if your work is to advise and organize, do it with care and enthusiasm. If it is to help the unfortunate, do it cheerfully.

Let your love be genuine, reject what is against love, take good hold of what assists it. Love each with a real brotherly affection, seeing who can do most to show the reverence we have for all men. Never let your willingness grow dim, let the spirit of love light up your whole life, as you hold yourselves at the service of love. Be happy, because love gives us hope, be patient in times of trouble, keep on wanting the victory of love. Do what you can for people in need, and make everyone welcome who comes to your houses.

Wish well even to those who treat you badly – wish them well, not ill. Try to be happy when others are, but share the sorrow of the unhappy. Live together without quarrels; shun the snobbish, but share the lives and concerns of ordinary people – never be priggish. Do your best not to get involved in disputes with other people, and never try to get your own back. If your enemy is hungry, feed him, if he's thirsty, give him a drink. This way you may get through his thick skin. Do not try to beat evil with more evil – it doesn't work. But you can destroy evil with love.

... Don't get into debt – except the debt of love we all owe each other. If we give love we have fulfilled all moral commands – they are all summed up in the phrase 'love your neighbour as yourself'.

It is high time you woke up. There is less time than we like to imagine.

Here is a very complete programme, and not an easy one. It is useful to end with such a ruthless spelling out of what it means to take love seriously. But this thoroughgoing union of love and technique is the way in which, as Socrates wanted, we may 'be enabled to bring forth, not images of beauty, but realities (for he has hold not of an image but of a reality) and bringing forth and nourishing true virtue to become the friend of God and be immortal, if mortal man may. Would that be an ignoble life?'

If not, as Paul says, it is high time we woke up to love.

BIBLIOGRAPHY

Author's Note: A list of books on, or relevant to, the subject of this one would fill another book. The following list is therefore highly selective, and is designed to be practically useful to the reader rather than comprehensive in scope.

There were three main criteria of selection, and one negative one.

1. These are books I have personally read. With such a wide field of choice this means there may well be excellent books not mentioned here, but I naturally cannot refer the reader to books which I either do not know of or have only a nodding acquaintance with.

2. These books, with one or two exceptions, are easily available. Many of them are currently obtainable in cheap paperback editions, the rest can be found in any public library of good size, or else on request in smaller ones.

3. They are comparatively readable. I have consulted some books not mentioned here which are either boring, or demand a specialized knowledge of a specialist subject.

4. I have omitted some books relevant to the subject which, although well known, I consider to be unscholarly, dishonestly tendentious, or just plain bad.

Books are divided under chapter subjects, but several refer to more than one chapter; I have not repeated their titles.

General

PLATO, *Symposium* (trans. Hamilton), Penguin, 1951
MCCABE, HERBERT, *Law, Love and Language*, Sheed & Ward, 1969
STORR, ANTHONY, *The Integrity of Personality*, Pelican, 1963
HAUGHTON, ROSEMARY, *On Trying to be Human*, Geoffrey Chapman, 1966

HAUGHTON, ROSEMARY, *The Transformation of Man*, Geoffrey Chapman, 1967

Chapter I

MEAD, MARGARET, *Male and Female*, Pelican, 1962
MEAD, MARGARET, *Growing up in New Guinea*, Pelican, 1963
MEAD, M, and WOLFENSTEIN (eds.) *Childhood in Contemporary Cultures*, Chicago U. Press, 1955
ROE, GORDON, *The Victorian Child*, Phoenix, 1959
BOWLBY, JOHN, *Child Care and the Growth of Love*, 2nd ed., Pelican, 1965
CARTER, MICHAEL P., *Into Work*, Pelican, 1966

Chapter II

NIETSZCHE, *Selections*, Viking Portable Library
WOOD, ERNEST, *Yoga*, Pelican, 1965
MOORE, GEORGE, *Esther Waters*
MALINOWSKI, *Sex and Repression in Savage Society*, Routledge, 1927
BINDER, PEARL, *Muffs and Morals*, Harrap, 1953
STENTON, D. M., *English Society in the Early Middle Ages*, Pelican History of England, 1965
MYERS, A. R., *England in the Late Middle Ages*, Pelican History of England, 1963
COHN, NORMAN, *The Pursuit of the Millennium*, Secker, 1957
HUGHES, PENNETHORNE, *Witchcraft*, Pelican, 1965
ROLLE, RICHARD, *The Amending of Life*, Orchard Books
STERN, KARL, *The Flight from Woman*, Allen & Unwin, 1966

Chapter III

DANIELSON, B., *Love in the South Seas*, Allen & Unwin, 1956
DE ROUGEMONT, *Passion and Society*, revised ed., Faber, 1956
MACMURRAY, *Reason and Emotion*, 2nd ed., Faber, 1962
SHIDELER, M. M., *The Theology of Romantic Love*, Harper, 1962
   (*Note*: This American book is not easily available here but is unique of its kind.)

THOMPSON, E. P., *The Making of the English Working Class*, New ed., Pelican, 1968

CORNFIELD (ED.), *Pictorial Biblical Encyclopedia*, Collier-Macmillan, 1964

HAMBLETT, C., and DEVERSON, J., *Generation X*, Gibbs & Phillips, 1964

GENET, JEAN, *The Thief's Journal*, Penguin, 1967

STRASSBURG, GOTTFRIED VON, *Tristan*, Penguin

COMFORT, ALEX, *Sex in Society*, Duckworth, 1963

VANN, GERALD, *To Heaven with Diana*, Collins, 1960

OLDENBOURG, ZOE, *The Cornerstone*, Gollancz, 1954

Chapter IV

BURNETT, FRANCES HODGSON, *Little Lord Fauntleroy*

BAGNOLD, ENID, *National Velvet*, Peacock Books

HOPKINS, A. B., *Elizabeth Gaskell: Her Life and Work*, Lehmann, 1952

MOLESWORTH, MRS., *Carrots, Herr Baby* and many others

WRIGHT, ANDREW, *Jane Austen's Novels*, Peregrine Books, 1962

KIPLING, RUDYARD, *Something of Myself, Kim*, etc.

ST AUGUSTINE, *Confessions*, Sheed & Ward

LUTYENS, MARY, *Millais and the Ruskins*, Murray, 1967

Chapter V

EAGLETON, TERENCE, *The New Left Church*, Sheed & Ward, 1966

LIENHARDT, G., *Social Anthropology*, 2nd ed., Oxford, 1966

EVANS PRITCHARD, *Essays in Social Anthropology*, Faber, 1962

PHILLIPS, MARGARET, *Small Social Groups in England*, Methuen, 1965

WILLIAMS, RAYMOND, *The Long Revolution*, Pelican, 1965

WILLIAMS, RAYMOND, *Culture and Society*, Pelican, 1961

BERG, LEILA, *Risinghill, Death of a Comprehensive School*, Pelican, 1968

WILLISON, GEORGE, *Saints and Strangers*, new ed., Heinemann, 1966

LORENZ, KONRAD, *On Aggression*, Methuen, 1966

Chapter VI

HUMPHREYS, C., *Buddhism*, Pelican, 1968

JAMESON, STORM (ed.), *Diary of Ann Frank*, Pan, 1968

RHEINHOLD, H. A. (ed.), *The Spear of Gold. Revelation of the Mystics*, Burns, Oates, 1947

MERTON, THOMAS, *Seeds of Contemplation*, Burns, Oates

MERTON, THOMAS, *Conjectures of a Guilty Bystander*, Sheed & Ward, 1968

SACKVILLE WEST, VITA, *The Eagle and the Dove*, Michael Joseph, 1943

ZAHN, GORDON, *In Solitary Witness*, Geoffrey Chapman, 1966

LASKI, MARGHANITA, *Ecstasy*, Cresset Press, 1965

HAUGHTON, ROSEMARY, *Act of Love*, Geoffrey Chapman, 1969

INDEX